Your Psychology Dissertation

BIRMINGHAM CITY
University

Your Psychology Dissertation

Emily Harrison
Panagiotis Rentzelas

Los Angeles | London | New Delhi
Singapore | Washington DC | Melbourne

Los Angeles | London | New Delhi
Singapore | Washington DC | Melbourne

SAGE Publications Ltd
1 Oliver's Yard
55 City Road
London EC1Y 1SP

SAGE Publications Inc.
2455 Teller Road
Thousand Oaks, California 91320

SAGE Publications India Pvt Ltd
B 1/I 1 Mohan Cooperative Industrial Area
Mathura Road
New Delhi 110 044

SAGE Publications Asia-Pacific Pte Ltd
3 Church Street
#10-04 Samsung Hub
Singapore 049483

British Library Cataloguing in Publication data

A catalogue record for this book is available from the British Library

Typeset by: C&M Digitals (P) Ltd, Chennai, India
Printed in the UK
Printed on paper from sustainable resources

ISBN 978-1-5264-3847-8 (pbk)

At SAGE we take sustainability seriously. We print most of our products in the UK. These are produced using FSC papers and boards.
We undertake an annual audit on materials used to ensure that we monitor our sustainability in what we are doing.
When we print overseas, we ensure that sustainable papers are used, as measured by the PREPS grading system.

Contents

Meet the Authors (and your dissertation module co-ordinators)

Dr Emily Harrison is Lecturer in Psychology at Birmingham City University. Her main research interests are concerned with understanding how children acquire and develop literacy skills, namely reading, phonological awareness and speech rhythm sensitivity. Emily studied for her undergraduate degree at Coventry University, where she conducted her own dissertation in the area of reading development, investigating the relationship between reading skills and speech rhythm sensitivity. This led to her being offered a place to do a PhD in reading development at Coventry under the supervision of Professor Clare Wood. Emily was awarded her PhD in 2015, which investigated the effectiveness of rhythmic-based interventions for enhancing literacy skills. Since then, Emily has worked closely with local schools, publishers and researchers to continue and build upon her research portfolio. Emily has worked at Birmingham City University since September 2015, where she is currently the Year Tutor for the final year students on the BSc Psychology programme, and leads multiple modules on both the undergraduate and postgraduate courses.

'As dissertation coordinator, I hope to inspire young and developing researchers. I am looking forward to guiding you through the module and helping you to conduct a project that you can be proud of. The dissertation is something you should enjoy, so manage your time well, stick to formative deadlines, and don't underestimate how long each process will take. Each and every one of you has the potential to succeed – don't let me down!'. – Emily

Dr Panagiotis (Panos) Rentzelas is a Lecturer in Social Psychology at Birmingham City University. Prior to this appointment Panagiotis was employed as Post-Doctoral Research Fellow in Social Psychology at the University of Essex and as a Policy Advisor/Scientific Officer for an international organisation. Panagiotis holds a PhD in Psychology from the University of Nottingham and BSc (Hons) in Psychology from the University of Essex. Panagiotis' research lies in the area of experimental social psychology, cross-cultural and contextual cognitive differences and in human motivation. Panagiotis has done extensive research investigating individualism and collectivism as cultural, group and individual constructs in intrinsic motivation. Furthermore, he has been involved in research investigating the cognitive, behavioural and emotional effects of different existential and contextual environmental norms. Finally, Panagiotis has experience in a range of empirical techniques, ranging from questionnaire studies to the use of social neuroscience paradigms in the form of electroencephalography (EEG).

'I am really excited for the textbook that you are holding in your hands. It has been created keeping your needs in mind, and is designed exclusively for the Birmingham City University final year psychology students. It is a bespoke textbook only for you! One of the reasons that I am the Dissertation module coordinator is because I want to help you enjoy this module as much as I did when I was an undergraduate student and I was walking in your shoes! This is your best chance to put in practice everything that you have learned throughout your undergraduate studies and create a dissertation project that belongs to you. I hope that you will enjoy the module and this textbook.' – Panos

How this Book Works...

This textbook has been custom built exclusively for students taking the module PSY6016: Psychology Dissertation at Birmingham City University.

Some of the chapters have been prepared by the module team, and therefore contain information specific to this module. Other chapters have been chosen by your module leaders from existing textbooks by other authors, and have been included because of their relevance to the module content.

Prior approval has been sought from all authors whose work is included in this book. You should also refer to your module guide for specific module content and information on the module timeline, assessment dates, and marking criteria.

Welcome to Your Dissertation!

Harrison E. and Rentzelas P.

The dissertation is an independent research project and is ultimately the most important assessment you will complete while at university. You will need to be able to demonstrate an ability to work independently, to manage the relationship with your supervisor, and to conduct an ethical and well-constructed research project that meets the following learning outcomes:

1. Demonstrate an understanding of the key concepts in producing a dissertation document, including structure, theme, presentation of literature sources, hypothesis, data collection, ethics, critique, discussion, conclusion and referencing.
2. Identify, appraise and critique key research papers and articles which logically rationalise a research project and compose conclusions and future areas of development.
3. Initiate, design, conduct (use psychological tools, specialist software and laboratory equipment where necessary) and report on the research project independently with academic support when needed.
4. Employ appropriate research methodology and data and statistical analysis.
5. Reflect on and employ ethical guidelines appropriately within the proposal, research methodology and collection of data which has been approved by the Psychology and or Faculty Ethics Committee.

The dissertation builds upon prior learning from Research Methods modules from Levels 4 and 5, and will encourage you to compile a research proposal which adheres to the Psychology/Faculty Ethics Committee and seek out research sources to produce an in-depth dissertation that answers their own identified research question or knowledge gap. All of the modules throughout this course will also help students when thinking about a topic area within psychology that they would like to concentrate on within this module.

This will be facilitated by you providing critical evaluation of the sources they have selected and used. You will also be facilitated in using statistical and other specialist software as well as the use of the psychology laboratories according to the needs of your project. Our lab technicians are there to help you with all the lab based and specialised needs of your dissertation project.

Understanding of research issues is an essential skill for psychologists operating in an evidence-based paradigm, and the ability to produce an in-depth dissertation and present a logical argument using such research is crucial and which is expected form a successful psychology graduate.

Support

Throughout the module, your dissertation coordinators will be providing you with lectures, workshops and writing sessions that will allow you to gain all the relevant information and guidance on preparing the proposal, writing your literature review, planning your methodology, applying for and gaining ethical approval, collecting your data, analysing your data, APA formatting, and putting it all together in the final dissertation.

As well as your module coordinators, you will also be allocated a supervisor who will be able to provide more targeted support. You are allowed 4 hours of project supervision, which you can use as and when you feel you need it. The supervisor's role is to oversee the general process of conducting a dissertation, as well as providing support through meetings, emails, and formative feedback.

Assessment

The dissertation module has two points of assessment:

1. **The Proposal (20%) (1,000 words) and completed ethics form (excluded from word count).**
   The first item of assessment is the research proposal. The proposal is 1,000 words in length and comprises a short literature review, plan of the methodology, and data analysis strategy. The proposal is worth 20% of the module mark and assesses LOs 1, 2, & 5.
2. **The Final Dissertation (80%) (7,000-10,000 words)**
   The second item of assessment is the final dissertation. This can be anything between 7,000–10,000 words in length, and contributes 80% of the final module mark. The final dissertation assesses LOs 1, 2, 3, 4 & 5.

You should make sure that you work from the detailed marking criteria provided in your module guide, as this will be used by module staff when marking your work. The detailed assessment marking criteria explains what we expect from an assessed piece of work, and this has been put in place to support and help you when preparing for assessments. When attaining feedback for summative assessments, your feedback will be based on standard clauses taken from these criteria. In order to be as transparent as possible, this is presented as a grid. Placed across the marking criteria you will have each grade banding and placed to the side you will have each learning outcome being assessed. This should help you to understand what you need to do for the summative assessment in order to achieve a particular grade for each learning outcome. This has been designed so that students are clear with their assessment preparation and that there is no ambiguity relating your work to the mark awarded. The benefit of a detailed assessment marking criteria also means that if you have more than one marker on the module, each marker will base their marking and feedback on this set detailed assessment marking criteria.

Please check your module guide for the up to date marking criteria and for deadline dates for the current academic year.

Module structure

The dissertation is a double module, meaning that it runs in both term 1 and term 2, and the module has been carefully structured in a way that allows you to complete one section at a time, minimising stress (hopefully!) and helping you to manage your time effectively. Specific dates for each item can be found in your module guide.

Lecture 1: Welcome to your dissertation
The first lecture will introduce you to the module and explain how the module will be run. Reading this chapter is a great start to understanding the module! Make sure you take a look at your module guide, too!

Lecture 2: The proposal and literature review
The second lecture will introduce you to your first summative piece of assessment on the module; the project proposal. The proposal should provide a general overview of what you plan to do, and should demonstrate that you are ready to begin working on your project. As such, you need to demonstrate that you have knowledge of the research literature, that you have planned your methodology, and that you know what tools you will use to collect your data. Chapters 2, 3, 4 & 5 of this book will be useful in helping you to plan your project.

Lecture 3: The ethical approval process
The third lecture will discuss the process of applying for and gaining ethical approval. You will need to submit a draft of your ethical approval application with the proposal, as a way of demonstrating that you have an understanding of ethical considerations. This lecture will guide you through the application form and will also highlight common ethical issues in dissertation projects. Chapter 6 of this book will help you to prepare your ethics application.

Lecture 4: Data collection tips
The fourth lecture will focus on data collection, an important phase in the dissertation. The lecture will be relevant to all projects, and will cover processes of data collection online and face-to-face, one-to-one and in groups and qualitative and quantitative.

Lecture 5: APA
The fifth lecture will cover information on APA formatting and referencing, including presentation of information, layout, writing style, grammar, in-text citations and the reference list. Chapter 7 of this book will cover some details on writing style. You should consult the APA publication manual for further advice on formatting, referencing and presentation.

Lecture 6: Formatting and submitting your dissertation
The sixth and final lecture will cover some tips on formatting the final dissertation document. The session will outline the order of sections, presentation of the final dissertation, and details on how to submit your work. Chapters 8 & 9 of this book will help you prepare the final document. Chapter 11 also contains some frequently asked questions which may be useful in helping you to overcome any issues which might arise.

Drop in sessions
Drop in sessions between your lectures will give you the opportunity to ask questions and gain clarification on each section of the dissertation.

Formative deadlines
The module has been structured in a way that allows you to focus on one section of the dissertation at a time. As such, we have se formative deadlines throughout the module that will give you the opportunity to gain formative feedback on the following:

- Proposal
- Methodology
- Literature review
- Data analysis and results

The only section that you will not gain any formative feedback on is the Discussion chapter. Please consult your module guide for individual submission dates.

The writing retreat

The writing retreat will take place in March of each academic year. At times, we recognise that it can be difficult to devote time to the dissertation, especially when you are already working on multiple other modules and assessments. The writing retreat offers an opportunity to take a day out from University and focus solely on the dissertation and nothing else. The day comprises workshops, support sessions, individual meetings, writing time and more, and is open to everybody who would like to attend. More information on the writing retreat will be communicated in your lectures and on Moodle.

2 Choosing a Topic and the Research Proposal

Evans, J.

Objectives

On reading this chapter you should:

- understand the importance of choosing a research topic that lends itself to a 'do-able' project;
- be able to evaluate potential topics;
- be able to formulate a valid research question (and hypothesis);
- understand the importance of creativity, and its relationship to innovation in formulating your research question;
- understand the integral role played by the research question;
- understand the vital role of the research proposal;
- be aware of the common pitfalls to be avoided in writing a successful proposal; and
- be able to write a logical and persuasive research proposal.

Overview

Chapter 3 deals with the practical issues of choosing an appropriate topic for your research project, and with the all important task of developing a research proposal. Section 3.1 deals with the practicalities of evaluating topics from your potential list, in order to choose the most appropriate for your project. Section 3.2 focuses on how to formulate a good research question. The role of the research question and different types of questions are dealt with in Section 3.3. Section 3.4 highlights the functional importance of the research proposal, which is often neglected by undergraduate students. The proposal acts as an exercise in thought, a reference point for supervision, and also as a motivational device. Section 3.5 deconstructs the proposal into its major components in order to make the development of the proposal more manageable. Section 3.6 presents the issue of the writing style of the proposal. Section 3.7 looks at some common pitfalls in developing a good proposal, while Section 3.8 provides a checklist for developing your research question and proposal.

3.1 Choosing a Topic

Often students adopt idealistic goals for their psychology project, due to the competition for good grades and for postgraduate places. You may want to make a significant contribution to the psychological literature, or you may want to publish your work; these are both very important and useful goals, but they should not override the importance of a 'do-able' project.

Often students want to research very broad, all-encompassing topics. Such broad topics involve more time and effort than most undergraduate psychology students can afford. However, topics that are too narrow should also be avoided as it is very difficult to generalise such results. You must strike a balance; your topic should be narrow enough to focus your project but not too narrow that the results have no generalisability. Also, your topic should be broad enough to generalise but not to the extent that you cannot manage the area and your project.

Simple strategies for evaluating potential research topics

It is quite common for undergraduate psychology students to develop a list of potential research topics. The difficulty arises when students must choose a topic from their list, and develop a research proposal. Often students ask me if they can submit two or three proposals, with the hope that I will inform them of the best idea and therefore make the decision for them. Supervisors are generally not in a position to do this, as it is unethical for anyone but the student to make this decision – this decision-making is, in itself, part of the research process. The following are three very essential questions that you can ask yourself regarding your potential research topics, as illustrated in Figure 3.1.

1. Does the topic elicit interest and curiosity in you?

The first decision you should make regards how you actually feel about the topics on your list, and whether you could stick with the topic through to the completion of a research project. It is very important that the topic you choose is of interest to you and that it also elicits curiosity within you. Your interest and curiosity should manifest themselves by adding to your enthusiasm about your project, and therefore have the potential to act as a powerful motivational device.

2. Is the topic worthwhile?

It is very important that you pick a topic that is worthwhile. As already noted in Chapter 2, poor science is unethical. It is unethical to ask people to participate

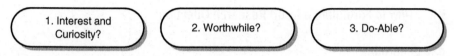

Figure 3.1   Three simple strategies for evaluating a potential research topic

in your study if it has little or no likelihood, because of poor conceptualisation and design, of producing meaningful results or furthering scientific knowledge.

If your topic is not worthwhile, not only is it unethical, but you are also failing to satisfy the requirements of meaningful results with theoretical and practical implications. Hence, you will fail to meet the full requirements for an undergraduate project in psychology, and you will ultimately lose precious marks. If the examiner of your project reads your project and thinks 'Well, so what?', then you have not met the full requirements of your psychology project. It is important to note that it is your responsibility to come up with valid topics that are worthwhile. Your supervisor's role is to guide you through the research process, not to generate topics for you.

3. Is the topic do-able?

As recently noted, it is of paramount importance that the topic for your project is feasible. You must make critical decisions regarding whether you will be capable of collecting primary data to answer your potential research question. For example, students are often interested in topics related to psychopathologies, such as schizophrenia or multiple personality disorders; however, at undergraduate level, it is not appropriate or permissible to gather information from such a sample, due to the code of competent caring for example.

A topic that Irish students are often interested in is the prison service. They may want to investigate inmates' quality of life, or they may be interested in the prison staff. At undergraduate level, students have great difficulty in gaining access to such sensitive samples, regardless of the aims of their study. Some students, due to family connections, etc., go through the process of getting permission to get into such places, and can spend numerous weeks waiting for a response, which is usually 'no'. Precious time is lost, which would have been saved by making critical decisions as mentioned above.

It is also important to decide whether you would have enough time to gather the information and carry out your analyses. Undergraduate students, for example, often do not have the time or resources to invest in participant observation studies, and should settle for some other method of inquiry that suits their research goals. Once you have narrowed down your list of topics, the next step in setting down the foundations for a successful psychology project is to develop your research question.

3.2   How to Formulate a Good Research Question

Idea generating

As already noted, all research begins with an idea, which can be the most difficult stage of the research process. Leonard and Swap (1999) define creativity as a process of developing and expressing novel ideas that are likely to be useful. Creativity is very important in considering the process of generating hypotheses for your psychology project, because generating your research question, like generating knowledge, is a creative act (Vicari & Troilo, 2000).

Generating a new idea is the beginning, not the end, of the creative process. Novelty for its own sake may result in nothing more than an intellectual exercise. Creativity is therefore an essential part of innovativeness, the starting point of a process which when skilfully managed brings an idea into innovation, (Leonard & Swap, 1999). Creativity is the process of imaginative thinking (*input*), which produces new ideas (for example the research question and hypothesis) while innovations are the *output*, in this case the completed psychology project.

Popper (1959) notes that there is no logical path leading to new ideas – they can only be reached by 'emfuhlung', i.e. creative intuition. However, it is important to note that creativity is more than just dreaming up grand ideas, insights and problems; the solutions to these problems must be original and feasible. This again highlights the importance of a do-able project in developing a research question where the solution is in fact feasible.

Leonard and Swap (1999) propose five steps that capture the essential features of the creative process, as seen in Figure 3.2.

It should come as no surprise that creativity comes from a well-prepared mind and so *Stage 1* of the process is preparation. There also needs to be an opportunity for innovation to occur, which is *Stage 2* of the creative process. The generating of your research question is a prime example of a need to exercise creativity. *Stage 3* involves the importance of generating as many initial ideas as possible. Creative ideas can begin with vague thoughts, and initial ideas can emerge in both scientific and non-scientific ways. In this early idea-getting phase, one should not be too critical of initial ideas because premature criticism might destroy an emerging good idea. The old saying rings through here – you shouldn't throw the baby out with the bathwater.

Cryer (2000) proposes numerous useful ways of generating options at this early phase in the creative process, as illustrated in Table 3.1 below.

Stage 4 of the process involves incubation: Leonard and Swap (1999) recognise the need for time out from struggling with an idea or issue. *Stage 5* involves selecting an idea from your generated list. Early ideas need to be nourished, thought about and taken seriously. Curiosity, interest and enthusiasm are critical ingredients. Once an area of interest is identified, it is useful to dive right in by reading articles and relevant books in the area.

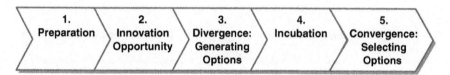

Figure 3.2   The creative process in five steps (Leonard and Swap, 1999)

Table 3.1   Strategies for generating creative ideas (Cryer, 2000)

1. Talking things over
2. Keeping an open mind
3. Brainstorming
4. Negative brainstorming
5. Viewing the problem from imaginative perspectives
6. Concentrating on anomalies
7. Focusing on byproducts
8. Viewing the problem from the perspective of another discipline

Using the research literature to generate ideas

As already noted, ideas for your research project often come out of the research literature. At this early stage in the research process, students are often intimidated by the vast amount of information available, and sometimes find themselves lost amidst the literature fog. There are a number of ways to approach the research literature; you could select a small number of topics within psychology which are of interest to you, and investigate them in depth. For example, a researcher may have an interest in children's reasoning but no particular idea for a research project. The interest, however, is enough to point the researcher to an area within which more defined ideas can be developed. For the new researcher in particular, interest in the area to be studied is critical in helping to sustain the hard work to follow. Remember the point about curiosity helping to generate ideas and sustain effort.

Another strategy is to acquaint yourself with research at the cutting edge of psychological knowledge. This can be achieved by keeping yourself up to date with top journals dedicated to your area of interest. For example, if your area of research is memory, it would be important to check each new issue of *The Journal of Experimental Psychology: Learning, Memory and Cognition*. A final strategy is to start with general readings such as the *Annual Review of Psychology*, and progress to more specific journal articles. Research questions can also develop from finding gaps in the literature, by attempting to refute or prove an existing theory, through everyday observations of behaviour, or from the need to solve a practical problem, as illustrated in Figure 3.3.

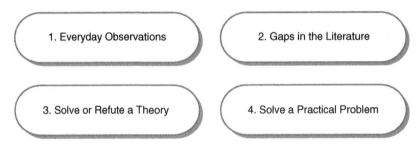

Figure 3.3   Sources for development of your research question

3.3   Clarifying and Refining your Research Question

The next stage involves clarifying and refining your ideas into research questions, as vague ideas are insufficient in psychology as a science. This process usually involves examining the research literature, in an attempt to learn how other researchers have conceptualised, measured and tested the concepts that are of interest to you and related to your ideas. While reviewing the literature, you will continue to work on your ideas, clarifying, defining and refining them, until you have produced one or more clearly posed questions based on a well-developed knowledge of previous research and theory, as well as on your own ideas and speculations.

The research question plays a vital role throughout the research process. It is vital that you present a clear statement of the specific purposes of your study. The research question simply formulates this specific purpose as a question. In writing the introduction section of your research project, your review of the literature must be defined by your research question which acts as the guiding concept.

Careful conceptualisation and phrasing of the research question is of paramount importance, because everything done in the remainder of the research process is aimed at answering your research question. The question that you develop might involve highly specific and precisely defined hypotheses typical of quantitative research. Or it might be phrased in a much more general manner typical of qualitative research. To a large extent, the research question that is posed will dictate the way you conduct the rest of the research process. This crucial aspect cannot be stressed enough: remember that throughout the grading of undergraduate projects, one fundamental issue is addressed when reading each section of the research: was that appropriate for the research question being asked? Students often fail to see this cardinal relationship at the early stages of the project, which can cause difficulties later on in the process.

1. Existence Questions

Example: Is there such a thing as the unconscious?

2. Descriptive and Classification Questions

Example: What are the personality characteristics of parents who slap their children?

3. Comparative Questions

Example: Are males better at mental rotation than females?

4. Composition Questions

Example: What are the factors that make up intelligence?

5. Relationship Questions

Example: Is body image related to self-esteem?

6. Causality Questions

Example: What are the effects of exercise on reaction time?

Figure 3.4   Different types of research questions (Meltzoff, 1999)

Different types of research questions

During this early stage of the research process, one works from the general to the specific using rational and abstract processes to systematically develop ideas towards valid research questions. In successfully asking questions, a very important requirement must be met. The question must be answerable with data; without this crucial caveat of testability, research questions are nothing more than a speculation.

Meltzoff (1999) illustrates that there are a number of different types of research questions that call for different methods of inquiry in seeking answers. Figure 3.4 illustrates these different types of research questions.

Evaluating your research question

One of the biggest difficulties for undergraduate students, at this stage of the research process, is that they are unsure whether their idea and research question are good enough, and whether they meet the requirements of originality and significance. If you have been having such feelings of doubt and uncertainty, you are certainly not alone. Originality can be achieved in a number of ways. First of all your research question can be original, or you may design your methodology in an original fashion, and finally your solution or answer to your research question may be original. Originality also arises from solving gaps in the literature, or by finding evidence for or against an existing theory using a novel or new method of inquiry. Originality can also arise from solving a practical problem in a new way, or a practical problem that did not have a solution.

Significance refers to whether your idea and research question are worthwhile. As already noted, in order to be worthwhile your research question should yield valid and meaningful results or findings, which will add to the existing knowledge base in psychology. The thought processes involved in developing your research proposal can aid in determining whether your research question is original and significant.

3.4 The Role of the Research Proposal

Your research proposal describes what your proposed research is about, what it is trying to achieve, how you will go about achieving it, what you find out and why it is worth finding out (Punch, 2001). Often undergraduate students under-estimate the importance of the research proposal, and fail to see the vital functions that it serves. This section highlights the functional importance of the research proposal, as seen in Figure 3.5.

An exercise in thought

The research proposal serves a number of useful functions. The most pertinent is that it helps you to think through each step of your research project. By writing the proposal you essentially have the opportunity to try out ideas, be creative and explore alternatives, without recruiting a single participant. If you

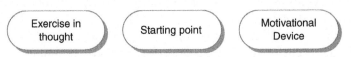

Figure 3.5   Functional importance of the research proposal

have a few ideas for your psychology project, you can write up a proposal for each one, and compare and evaluate them, to help you choose the most viable idea. This useful writing process also helps you make intelligent and ethical research decisions.

Starting point for supervision

The research proposal can serve as a very effective reference place for your supervision. The proposal also allows your supervisor to think through your research plan so that they can give advice that will improve your study. On the other hand if your supervisor is unsure of your research focus, or of the relevance of your research question, a well-written proposal allows them to make a more concrete informed decision regarding its approval. Remember that a well-written research proposal could convince your supervisor that your research is worthwhile, and that you have the competence to carry it out.

Motivational device

The research proposal can also help you stay on the right track, and act as a powerful motivational device. The undergraduate research project is a timely endeavour – once you have embarked on this journey, it is possible to loose track or become disheartened. Returning to the proposal can remind you of the potential contribution your project could make to psychology as a science, and to the practical applications that could ensue. Chapter 5 deals with motivation and your psychology project in more detail.

3.5   The Research Proposal Deconstructed

Undergraduate students often find the development of an effective research proposal for quantitative and qualitative projects an exasperating and difficult experience. This section deconstructs the proposal into its major components, as seen in Figure 3.6, in order to make the development of the proposal more manageable and practical.

1. Statement of the research problem

It is vital that your present a clear statement of the specific purposes of your study. It is important that you also explain, very clearly, why your research question is worth answering. What do you hope to learn from it? What will this new knowledge add to the existing field? What new perspective will you bring to the topic? For quantitative research you must also very explicitly

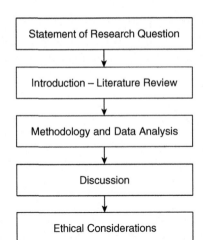

Figure 3.6   Components of the research proposal for both quantitative and qualitative research (Note: not all universities require a discussion section)

state your hypothesis(es). This is the tentative prediction of the answer to your research question. Sometimes students assume that their hypotheses are obvious, and do not state them. This is a major mistake, which should be avoided at all costs. No matter how obvious your hypotheses appear, it is imperative that you state them. Clear hypotheses are very important, as the rest of the quantitative research process is geared towards establishing confirmation of them.

2. Introduction – literature review

The literature review is generally incorporated into the introduction. The main purpose of this section is to provide the necessary background or context for your research problem. The framing of the research question is the most crucial aspect of the research proposal. If you frame your research question in the context of a general long-winded literature review, the significance of your research question could ultimately be lost and appear inconsequential or uninspiring. However, if you frame your research question within the framework of a very focused and current research area, its importance will be markedly apparent.

The literature review demonstrates your knowledge and understanding of the theoretical implications of your research question. It demonstrates your ability to critically evaluate relevant research, and illustrates your ability to integrate and synthesise information. Try to outline conflicting research in the area that your project will try to resolve. Most importantly, the literature review convinces your supervisor that your proposed research project will make a substantial contribution to psychology as a science. For the reasons mentioned, even qualitative proposals require a literature review; however, you need to strike a balance between adequate knowledge to focus your study, and immersing too much in the literature that your study becomes too contaminated with prior expectations. This idea is dealt with in more detail in Chapter 8.

3. Methodology

Your methodology is very important because it illustrates how you plan to answer your research question. It acts as a work plan and describes how you will complete your project. It is crucial that you include sufficient information for your supervisor to ascertain if your methodology is sound and demonstrates scientific rigour. Quantitative and qualitative methodologies do not lend themselves to the same description and will therefore be dealt with separately in more detail in Units 2 and 3 of the text.

Quantitative methodology

Design – What are your independent variable(s) and dependent variable(s)? It is very important that these are operationally defined, using precise and concise language. Also mention how you propose to measure them. What type of design do you propose to answer your research question(s)?

Participants – How will you choose your sample? Do you foresee any difficulties accessing this sample? Are there any limitations to using such a sample?

Materials – Describe the type of equipment and materials you plan to use.

Procedure – Explain, in as much detail as you can, how you propose to conduct your research.

Statistical considerations – Although you have no results as yet, it is important that you demonstrate an understanding of the statistical analyses that will answer your research question. It is imperative that you suggest procedures that are appropriate considering the type of design you propose to utilise and the type of data that you will collect. For example, if you are comparing two different groups, and have proposed an independent groups design, then, if it is interval/ratio data, an independent t-test would be appropriate, but if the data was categorical, then a χ^2 would be appropriate to answer the research question.

Qualitative Methodology

Silverman (2003) notes the importance of the theoretical underpinnings of the methodology chosen, and the contingent nature of the data chosen in qualitative research. Your research paradigm, for example grounded theory, should be included in your proposal. Explain the assumptions of your research paradigm.

Qualitative methodology should deal with a description of the cases chosen, the procedures for data collection and analysis in terms of their suitability to the theoretical framework applied and how they satisfy criteria of reliability and validity (Silverman, 2003). It is important to realise that in qualitative research, data collection and data analysis often occur simultaneously.

4. Discussion of potential findings

It is important to note that not all universities require a discussion section in the research proposal. It is advisable that you check the polices of your university to ascertain whether this section is necessary. In my view, it is beneficial that you discuss the potential impact of your proposed research project. This can be communicated in a few sentences, the goal of which is to demonstrate to your supervisor that you believe in your project.

5. Ethical considerations

As already noted in Chapter 2, planned steps must always be taken to protect and ensure the dignity and welfare of all your participants, and that inadequate attention for respect and beneficence can affect the scientific viability and validity of your proposed research. It is also crucial that you demonstrate an active concern for the well-being of your participants, by minimising potential harms and maximising the benefits of participating in your study. It is very important that all participants are volunteers, and have given informed consent to take part. It is also important to map out how you will uphold these ethical obligations.

3.6   A Note on Writing Style

It is important to keep in mind that your proposal is an argument. An effective research proposal, therefore, should be clear and precise, be persuasive and convincing, and demonstrate the broad implications of the research (Silverman, 2003). One of the benefits of viewing your proposal as an argument is that such a structure pushes you to stress your thesis or line of thought. This structure also requires that your arguments and statements are consistent with each other. One of the main aims of the popular writing and publication formats is clarity of communication. This very much parallels with the principle of parsimony, which is applied to science in general. Cryer

(2000) proposes that the research proposal should use language and terminology that is understandable to an intelligent lay person as well as to a subject matter expert.

Silverman (2003) warns that you should never be content with a proposal which reads like a stream of undigested theories or concepts. It is crucial that you use precise and concise language that a non-specialist can understand. By explaining all relevant concepts and variables, you will have demonstrated the ability to write and think clearly and critically. Remember that your research proposal is your supervisor's best way of getting a sense of your thinking, and it illustrates that your research project itself will be organised in the same logical way. Morse (1994a) highlights the importance of a well-thought-out proposal in noting that a sloppily prepared proposal sends the message that the actual research itself may also be sloppy. It is very important that you are convincing of the practical importance of your research project, and that you develop a sufficient contextual basis for your research problem.

3.7   Common Pitfalls

Students often have difficulty in writing a research proposal that gains the support of their supervisor and their university's ethics review board. The following are some common mistakes made in proposal writing.

1. Vague presentation of your research problem.
2. Framing your research problem within a long-winded literature review.
3. Failure to demonstrate the significance of your research proposal.
4. Vague methodology and proposed handling of your results.
5. Inadequate consideration of ethics for psychological research.
6. Poor writing style which lacks clarity and precision.

3.8   Checklist

- Does your research question address an original and significant psychological phenomenon? 'An original contribution to knowledge' does not mean that it must explore a new problem; it can also result from a novel reassessment of a familiar question.
- Is your research question clear?
- Can your research question be answered by data?
- Have you developed a clear, persuasive and comprehensive research proposal that will guide you through the research process?
- Is your research question consistent with each aspect of your proposal?
- Does your proposal explain the logic behind your proposed investigation as opposed to merely describing it?

Summary

There are some simple strategies for evaluating potential research topics, for example deciding whether a topic elicits your interest and curiosity, whether the topic is worthwhile to investigate and whether it is feasible. Creativity and innovation are important in generating a valid research question. Creativity can be viewed as the process of imaginative thinking (*input*) which produces new ideas, while innovations, in this context your research question and your psychology project, are the *output*. The research literature is also important in generating ideas. The careful conceptualisation and phrasing of the research question is critical, as everything done in the remainder of the research process is aimed at answering that question.

The research proposal acts as a useful exercise in thought, allowing you to think critically through each aspect of the research proposal and to make necessary ethical decisions. The research proposal also serves as a very effective starting point for supervision, and also acts as a powerful motivational device. Both qualitative and quantitative research proposals can be broken down into the statement of the research question, the introduction-literature review, methodology and data analysis, discussion and ethical considerations. There are a number of mistakes often made by undergraduate students, from hazy presentation of the research problem, to poor writing style. A clear, precise and persuasive writing style is critical in demonstrating the practical and theoretical significance of your project, and in demonstrating your ability to think and plan in a logical, rigorous manner.

Further Reading

Cryer, P. (2000) *The Research Student's Guide to Success.* Buckingham: Open University Press. (Aimed at post-graduate level. Details useful creative strategies.)

Punch, K. F. (2001) *Developing Effective Research Proposals.* London: Sage Publications.

Silverman, D. (2003) *Doing Qualitative Research: A Practical Handbook.* London: Sage Publications.

3

The Research Project as a Means of Acquiring Knowledge

Evans, J.

Objectives

On reading this chapter you should:

- understand how psychology operates as a scientific discipline;
- understand the role of the undergraduate psychology project as a means of acquiring knowledge; and
- be aware of the usefulness of viewing qualitative and quantitative research situations as opposite ends of a continuum, as opposed to two distinctly separate approaches to inquiry.

Overview

Section 1.1 deals broadly with how psychology operates as a scientific discipline, and demonstrates how science can be viewed as a way of thinking (which involves asking and answering questions) and to produce more knowledge. Section 1.2 goes on to consider the psychology project as a means of acquiring knowledge. Section 1.3 deals with acquiring knowledge in psychology both quantitatively and qualitatively – it is proposed that it is useful to view the two approaches as research situations on opposite ends of a continuum, as opposed to two distinct approaches to research and inquiry within psychology. Finally Section 1.4 gives a brief overview of the importance of your research question in choosing a quantitative or qualitative method of inquiry.

1.1 What is the Purpose of Science for Psychology?

Often when people think of the word 'science', the first image that comes to mind is one of test tubes, computers and people in white laboratory coats. Some sciences, such as physics and chemistry, deal with the physical and material world, for example with chemicals and electricity. These natural sciences or hard sciences are generally the basis of new technology, and therefore receive a lot of publicity.

The social and behavioural sciences, such as psychology, sociology and anthropology, involve the study of people, including their beliefs, attitudes and behaviours. People do not always associate these disciplines with the word science, and are sometimes referred to as 'soft sciences'. The reference to soft does not mean that these disciplines lack scientific rigour or that they are sloppy or limp; it refers to their subject matter. Human behaviour and social life are far more fluid and transient than the tangible composites of chemistry and physics. However, the natural sciences are not made more scientific than psychology by virtue of their laboratory equipment. It is important to note that although many processes of inquiry produce scientific tools and products, it is the process of inquiry or way of thinking that encapsulates the essence of science.

The essence of science is this way of thinking. Science therefore encompasses a process of formulating specific questions, and finding answers to these questions, in order to gain a better understanding of phenomenon. These gains in our understanding produce and increase our knowledge base. This is reiterated by Chalmers' (1990) statement that science aims to produce knowledge of the world. Therefore, scientific research in psychology involves posing a question and then initiating a systematic process to obtain valid answers to that question. This process is carried out utilising the scientific method, which serves the basis for scientific inquiry. The overall goal of psychology as a science is to understand behaviour and phenomenon. Using the scientific method, understanding comprises four important goals of being able to *describe, predict, understand* and *control* behaviour or phenomena.

1.2   The Psychology Project as a Means of Acquiring Knowledge

The psychology project is an integral component of the undergraduate student's curriculum. Psychology departments continue this long tradition of inquiry, through the requirement of the final year project. The role of the research project is therefore a means of inquiry; through formulating questions and finding answers to them, students add to their knowledge base. Figure 1.1 depicts the cyclical recursive nature of the research process, and reflects the thinking process whereby new information results in new knowledge and understanding.

Through this process of inquiry, the primary purpose of the undergraduate psychology project is to provide the student with practice in asking and answering questions. In carrying out your project, you gain valuable experience and training in planning, conducting, analysing and presenting an independent

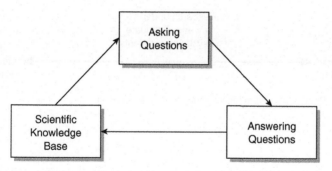

Figure 1.1   The scientific process of inquiry

research project. More specifically, you will develop the necessary skills involved in conducting library research, academic writing, designing research, collecting, analysing and interpreting data. Also, on a more general level, you will learn about the conventions and requirements of psychological research, which will equip you for post-graduate research, and for communication within the scientific field of psychology.

1.3   Quantitative and Qualitative Methods of Inquiry

A method is a systematic approach to a piece of research. Psychologists use a wide range of methods of inquiry. There are a number of ways in which the methods used by psychologists are classified, the most common being between quantitative and qualitative methods. Camic, Rhodes and Yardley (2004) note that it is time to abandon the view that what separates quantitative and qualitative approaches is whether to count or not to count, measure or not measure, sample or not sample. This view is supported by Shweder (1996, p. 179) because all social science research counts and measures in some way or another, the true difference is what to count and measure, and what one discovers.

It can therefore prove useful to view the quantitative and qualitative approaches to research in psychology as situations on opposite ends of a continuum representing the field of psychological research. Figure 1.2 illustrates that at one polar end of the continuum, there is pure quantitative research, apparent by clearly defined variables, theories and hypotheses. On the opposite end of the continuum is pure qualitative research in psychology, which relies on the subjective interpretation of cases and events. The qualitative and quantitative research undertaken by undergraduate students generally falls away from the polar ends of such a continuum. Quantitative research aims at having external as well as internal validity. Students also recognise the implications of very sterile laboratory conditions which are not transferable to real life settings, while qualitative research aims at making some contribution to

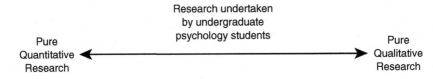

Figure 1.2   Continuum of qualitative and quantitative research

theory and application in general as opposed to developing a new theory for each case.

In between these two polar extremes, therefore, are numerous different approaches to research. With this in mind it is easier to see how both approaches may share some common ground with regard to psychology as a science. Qualitative research that investigates cases, which may be utterances, narratives, attitudes, phenomenon, events, etc., are comparable to quantitative research that investigates variables and constructs. This derivation arises from the idea that cases have the same analysable features as variables, and hence a shared scientific foundation exists. For example, cases can have varying characteristics, just like characteristics of a variable can vary. Therefore it is possible to investigate similarities and differences among such cases.

The debate as to whether quantitative and qualitative research methods can be complementary is ongoing. Although the two styles share basic principles of science, the two approaches differ in significant ways. Each has its strengths and weaknesses. I agree with King (1994) that the best research often combines features of both approaches, in order to build a more complete picture of the phenomenon. For example, there may be two stages in the same piece of research, with a qualitative approach yielding initial ideas which can then by investigated via a quantitative approach. This also coincides with Todd (2003) who has also noted that although the two approaches have traditionally been seen as competing paradigms, in recent years researchers have begun to argue that the divide is artificial. That the distinction between quantitative and qualitative can be a false one is obvious when they are viewed as two approaches to studying the same phenomena. However, the problem arises when they provide different answers (Clark-Carter, 2004). Nonetheless, the distinction can be a convenient device for classifying methods.

1.4   How to Choose the Appropriate Method of Inquiry: Quantitative or Qualitative?

Your choice of method of inquiry for your psychology project will largely rely on your research aims and your research question. The role of the research question will be dealt with in more detail in later chapters; however, it is beneficial at this point to briefly deal with the issue. For example, if you have developed a research question that addresses causes of behaviour, it will be appropriate to carry out an experimental research project in order to answer your research question. On the other hand, if your aims are to describe a phenomena from the participant's own frame of reference, then qualitative methods would usually be appropriate.

Imagine your goal is to refine an area within psychology that has already been thoroughly researched, in this situation you might want to use a tightly controlled experimental design to investigate a cause and effect. However, if you are researching a new area within psychology, you might decide on a more exploratory qualitative method. Also, if you are interested in people's behaviour, but not in their beliefs and intentions, an experiment might be appropriate. Or if you want to know the meaning that the behaviour has for the participant, then you may want to employ a qualitative method of inquiry.

Undergraduate students often use quantitative methods of inquiry, such as the true experiments, quasi-experiments, correlational and differential research. Some common qualitative methods of inquiry are semi-structured interviews, grounded theory and interpretative phenomenological analysis.

Summary

The essence of science is the systematic logic used in asking and answering questions, and producing more knowledge. The role of the research project is therefore a means of inquiry: through formulating questions and finding answers to them, students add to their knowledge base. It is useful to view quantitative and qualitative approaches to research as situations on opposite ends of a continuum, as opposed to two distinct approaches to research and inquiry in psychology. Whether you use a qualitative or quantitative method of inquiry for your project will largely depend on your research aims and your research question.

Further Reading

Camic, P., Rhodes, J. and Yardley, L. (eds) (2004) *Qualitative Research in Psychology: Expanding Perspectives in Methodology and Design*. Washington: APA.

Chalmers, A. (1990) *Science & its Fabrication*. Buckingham: Open University Press.

Ragin, C. (1987) *The Comparative Method: Moving Beyond Qualitative & Quantitative Strategies*. Berkeley and London: University of California Press.

Todd, Z., Nerlich, B., McKeown, S. and Clarke, D. (eds) (2004) *Mixing Methods in Psychology*. Hove and New York: Psychology Press, Taylor & Francis.

Understanding the Research Literature

Ness Evans, A., and Rooney, B. J.

OBJECTIVES

After studying this chapter, students should be able to

- Search the literature using common online databases
- Describe what is meant by the term *peer reviewed*
- List and describe what is contained in each section of a typical research article
- Define independent, dependent, participant, mediating, and moderating variables
- Identify important variables in a research article
- Describe the typical descriptive statistics found in research articles
- Understand at a conceptual level common parametric tests of significance used by researchers in the social sciences
- List common nonparametric alternatives to parametric tests of significance
- Understand how confidence intervals are used in estimating parameters

You have selected your research topic. Now, you need to discover what research has *already* been done on the topic. It is time for you to peruse the research literature. You will probably find some research on your topic, but it is unlikely that anyone has done exactly the same study that you have in mind. We often tell our students to think through their

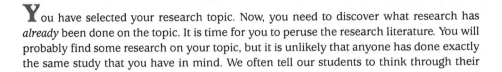

topic before going to the literature because it is easier to be creative about your project before you have looked at the other approaches. Indeed, once you have read a few articles in the area, it may be very difficult to think of an original idea!

Although it is unlikely that a study identical to yours has already been done, reading the literature will give you an idea about the kinds of problems that other researchers have had, and you can assess their solutions to those problems. The literature can provide a historical context for your study by describing what has been done and what remains to be explored. You will also find valuable information on how to measure variables, how to control variables, and, in experimental studies, how to manipulate variables. This sounds wonderful, but how do you start to search through all the research to find studies relevant to your topic? In the "good old days," this required many hours (or days) of wading through heavy indexes of research (just imagine a dozen or more telephone directories). Today, there are a number of computer indexes that require no heavy lifting.

SEARCHING THE LITERATURE

There are a number of bibliographic databases for the psychology literature, including Proquest, ERIC, and PsycINFO. We prefer PsycINFO, an index that is produced by the American Psychological Association and is probably the most widely used bibliographic search engine for English-language journals (http://www.apa.org/pubs/databases/psycinfo/index.aspx).

What is the *psychology literature*? When we use this term, we are usually referring to original research published in peer-reviewed journals. These journals can be easily recognized by their common layout. They begin with an abstract (a short summary) and include an *introduction*, a *method* section, a *results* section, and a *discussion*. But the literature also includes review articles, books, chapters in books, edited volumes, and chapters in edited volumes. These sources are not usually where original research is published. Rather, they usually provide a summary of a collection of research studies in a particular area. Although these sources can be useful in helping you put the research in context, it is better to read the original research and draw your own conclusions.

Not included in the list above are newspapers, magazines (including *Psychology Today*), and websites. There are two reasons why scientific research is not published in these media: (1) the presence of advertising and (2) the lack of peer review. Let's talk about advertising. Newspapers and magazines contain a lot of advertising of products and services. Indeed, these publications would not be viable without advertisers. Editors of newspapers and magazines must keep their advertisers happy; therefore, we, as consumers of the information in these publications, cannot be confident that reporting will be unbiased. Now, we are not saying that all newspaper and magazine reports are biased, but they could be. For example, imagine you have conducted a study that shows that drinking Brand X beer can lead to spontaneous, uncontrollable hiccupping. You send your report to a magazine that has Brand X beer as a major advertiser. It's pretty unlikely that the magazine editor will accept your paper for publication. Yes, your research might be terrific, but the potential damage to the advertiser in terms of sales of the product might lead the editor to reject your study for publication. This is why you will not see advertising in journals. Journal editors, by not permitting advertising, avoid the conflict of interest problem that advertising brings.

The second reason why original scientific research is not usually published in newspapers or magazines is that neither of these sources requires review of the research by expert peers. Some sources that you can search are peer reviewed, and some are not. It is important to understand the peer review process because it is a fundamental safeguard of quality in research. As the name implies, *peer review* is a process whereby the editor of a journal sends submitted manuscripts out to be reviewed by other researchers in the same field of study. The manuscript is read and critiqued by peers who have expertise in the area. The review is usually *blind*; this means that the name(s) of the author(s) of the manuscript is removed from the manuscript before the copies are sent to the peer reviewers. Blind review also means that the editor does not reveal the reviewers' names to the author(s) of the manuscript. Blind review helps guard against any personal conflicts that may be present among researchers and facilitates a fair review of the research. The editor receives the reviews and decides whether the paper should be accepted as submitted, accepted with minor changes, accepted with revisions, or not accepted at all. If the manuscript is accepted but changes are required, the author(s) is given the opportunity to make the changes necessary to satisfy the editor and to address the concerns of the reviewers. If the study has major flaws, it may have to be redone and resubmitted (of course, the researchers can submit the manuscript to another journal and hope for a more positive review).

Peer review helps maintain a high standard of quality in research. Without peer review, shoddy or even fraudulent research might be published that could send other researchers off on a wild-goose chase that could last for years. Keep in mind that books and magazines (e.g., *Psychology Today*) are usually not peer reviewed.

NOTE: In our courses, we do not permit the use of *Psychology Today* as a source. Students often question this because a lot of psychological research is reported in *Psychology Today*. Along with the advertising and peer review issues, which we discussed above, there are two other reasons for our decision to not permit this magazine as a source for student papers. One reason is simple—we do not want our students to use secondary sources of any kind. Second, the writers for *Psychology Today* are not scientists; they may have some academic background in the area, but they are writing for the magazine as reporters. *Psychology Today*, like any other magazine, needs to sell magazines. Articles written by reporters will not be published unless the editor believes that the report will help sales.

FYI

There are two notable exceptions to the "no ads in journals" rule. Ironically, the two most prestigious scientific journals worldwide are full of advertisements. *Science* and *Nature* are peer reviewed, highly respected, and widely circulated.

When you are ready to use a bibliographic database, your first step is to select the appropriate *search terms*. Often students will complain that they cannot find anything in the literature on a particular topic, even though a lot of research is there. Usually, the problem is that they have not used the correct terms when doing the search. Using the correct terms is crucial; fortunately, the databases have a thesaurus of *keywords* to help you.

Imagine you want to find articles on treating seasonal affective disorder (SAD) with light therapy. You can go directly to the thesaurus in PsycINFO and look for "seasonal affective disorder." You will find that the term is used in the database; you will see a brief definition of SAD and the information that the term was introduced in 1991. PsycINFO also provides broader terms that would include SAD and narrower terms that are relevant. One of the narrower terms is *phototherapy*. That sounds useful. You can select "phototherapy" by clicking on the box, and you can similarly select "seasonal affective disorder." The default is to connect these two phrases with "or," but if you want articles that contain both phrases, you should choose the "and" option. When you click "and" and search (DE "Seasonal Affective Disorder") and (DE "Phototherapy") you will find 276 publications with those keywords. You might want to limit your search to only peer-reviewed articles in English by clicking "refine search" and selecting *peer-reviewed journals* under *publication type*. Below that is a box for selecting the language, namely, English. If you select this and search again, you will get 235 hits. That's a more manageable number, but probably still more than you want to read. Let's limit the search to only *original journal articles* under *document type*. This time the search finds only 25 articles. That seems like a reasonable number. Now, you can click on each one and read the abstract of the article. The abstract is a short but comprehensive summary of the article, and based on your perusal of the abstracts, you can decide which articles you want to read in their entirety. If you have done the search the way we have described, you would find that the second article is titled "Light Therapy for Seasonal Affective Disorder With Blue 'Narrow-Band' Light-Emitting Diodes (LEDS)." This might be the one you choose to read. If your library has access to the full-text electronic version of the article, you will be able to download it immediately. If your library does not have access, then you will have to order a copy, called a reprint. You can also write to the principal investigator and request a reprint. This may take a while, so you should begin your *literature search* early. If you leave reprint requests until the last minute, you may not be able to get the articles that are most relevant to your research topic.

Here is another example. Suppose we are interested in how the color of a room might influence mood. A search using the terms *mood* and *room color* produces nothing. Perhaps *room* is too restrictive. A search with *mood* and *color* gives 237 articles. Now, let's refine (limit) the search to just peer-reviewed articles in English. Wow, still 167 articles. PsycINFO has a bar that reads "Narrow results by subject," and in the list there is "color." What happens if we click that? We get 31 articles that deal with color and mood—that's perfect! Apparently, this search requires that color be a keyword and not just a word that appears in the title or abstract. The fifth article in the list looks interesting; it is titled "Effects of Colour of Light on Nonvisual Psychological Processes" by Igor Knez at the University of Gävle, Sweden. Again, your library may or may not have access to the full text of the article. Be sure to consult with your reference librarians. These people are well educated and typically underutilized by students. If you have a question, ask your librarian.

THE RESEARCH ARTICLE

Now that you have a research article in hand, let's examine each section of the article separately. When reading the literature, you need to understand that each section has a purpose and contains specific types of information. Once you know how research articles are written, you will know which section will contain the information you need. The following discussion is presented to help you *read* the literature. You will find information on *writing* a research article in Chapter 14.

The Abstract

The abstract is a comprehensive summary of the article and describes what was done, to whom, and what was found. Online bibliographic search engines such as PsycINFO provide the title and the abstract. If the title seems relevant, you can read the abstract. It should provide you with enough information to decide whether you want to read the entire article.

The Introduction

The introduction directly follows the abstract. Here, the author(s) provides background on the research problem. You will find a description of the relevant research (this is the researcher's literature search) and how it logically leads to the research being reported in the article. Usually, near the end of the introduction, you will find a description of the research hypothesis of the author. Again, for information on *writing* an introduction, see Chapter 14.

Knez (2001) has an introduction with a typical layout. He begins with a general statement about the state of knowledge in the research area. He then presents a discussion of the previous research, organized by variables. He describes the various independent variables that have been identified as important and discusses various confounding variables and how these should be controlled. He also discusses a theoretical framework that is based largely on his own research. And finally, he defines the purpose of the present research, how it will solve some of the problems identified in the literature review, and why it is important.

Before we continue to a discussion of the method section, it is probably a good idea to review the types of variables you will read about in the introduction of many research articles.

Independent Variable

You will recall that an independent variable (IV) is the variable in an experiment that is manipulated by the researcher. The researcher chooses levels of the IV that he or she thinks will have effects on some response measure. The researcher then assigns participants to each level of the IV (or all levels in the case of repeated-measures designs) and compares the differences in response measures to see if the IV had an effect. You will recall that some variables are not true IVs. The values of these participant variables may be inherent in the participants. Examples include gender, age, disability type, and so on. Or participants might have self-selected the value of the variable. For example, differences in school success between children attending private and public schools is a comparison on a participant variable where the participants have, in effect, assigned themselves to the values of the variable. In either case, studies of group differences on participant variables are not true experiments; rather, they are *quasi-experiments*. Remember that a true IV is under the direct control of the researcher. The researcher chooses the values of the variable and assigns participants to each and then looks to see if that manipulation has any effect on their responses, the dependent variable. In an experiment, the IV can be thought of as the *cause* in a cause–effect relationship.

FYI

Statistical packages such as IBM® SPSS® Statistics Version 18.0 do not distinguish between true IVs and participant (or subject) variables. They refer to both as IVs.

Dependent Variable

The dependent variable (DV) in psychological research is some response measure that we think will be influenced by our IV. Reading comprehension might be a DV, and we might measure number correct on a comprehension quiz as our operational definition of reading comprehension. Or we might measure depression by having participants rate how they feel on a scale. In an experiment, the DV can be thought of as the *effect* in a cause–effect relationship.

When we are trying to determine patterns of responding by measuring variables, we are always concerned with the natural variability of participants' responses. Of course, our goal in research is to explain some of this variability. For example, if your research question is "Do students who read a lot understand better what they read?" then you are in a sense trying to account for the variability in student reading comprehension by determining how much they read. This is the variability that you are interested in explaining with your relationship. However, some variability is outside our primary interest. For example, if we are trying to determine if classroom technology improves learning, we are not interested in variables such as temperature of the classroom, time of day of the class, or ability of the instructor. Rather, we want to control or account for these variables so that we can better assess the effect of our primary variable (i.e., technology).

If other variables that might have affected the DV have been controlled in some way, then the researcher can conclude that differences in the DV are a result of, or caused by, the IV manipulation. This is the core of the experimental design, and to the degree that other variables have been controlled, we can be more confident in making causal inferences with these designs than we can from nonexperimental research. We discuss the various ways to control these other variables in Chapter 4.

CONCEPTUAL EXERCISE 2A

1. Identify the IVs and DVs for each of the following:

   a. Reaction time decreased when more practice trials were given.

   b. Amount of exercise had an effect on depression ratings.

Moderating Variables

Many cold remedies display warnings that they should never be taken with alcohol. It is often the case that these drugs can cause drowsiness, but this cause-and-effect relationship is increased with the consumption of alcohol. In this example, alcohol is acting as a moderating variable by amplifying the drowsiness effect of the drug. Moderating variables act to influence the relationship between the IV and the DVs. A moderating variable can increase, decrease, or even reverse the relationship between the IV and the DVs. If, as discussed above, the IV is the cause in the cause-and-effect relationship and the DV is the effect in the cause-and-effect relationship, then the moderating variable is a third influence that must be taken into account to clearly describe the cause-and-effect relationship. For example, in his famous studies on obedience, Milgram (1974) found that the actions of a confederate-companion (someone posing as a participant who is actually part of the study) could produce a strong moderating effect. When the confederate-companion agreed to shock the learner, 93% of the true participants continued to administer shocks, but when the confederate disobeyed the order, only 10% of the true participants continued.

In the Knez (2001) study of the effect of light on mood, gender was identified as a moderating variable. Relative to cool light, warm lighting produces a more positive emotional response in women than it does in men. Therefore, the influence that lighting has on mood is moderated by the gender of the participant.

In a recent study conducted in Islamabad, Altaf and Awan (2011) examined how spirituality moderates the relationship between office workload and job satisfaction. By surveying 76 employees, they assessed the relationship between workload, workplace spirituality, and level of job satisfaction. Workplace spirituality is a person's sense of meaning and purpose. They found that spirituality was positively related to job satisfaction, but they didn't find the negative relationship between workload and job satisfaction that had been reported in the literature (Khan, 1980, as cited in Altaf & Awan, 2011). They suggest that workplace spirituality moderates the usually negative effect of workload on job satisfaction. Essentially, if a workplace fosters an environment where employees find spiritual meaning, a heavy workload does not reduce job satisfaction. (For more discussion on moderating variables, see the discussion of factorial designs in Chapter 7.)

Direct relationship between IV and DV
For example,

IV   DV

Condom use   Sexually transmitted infections (STIs)

Condom use is directly related to incidence of STD in sexually active young people.

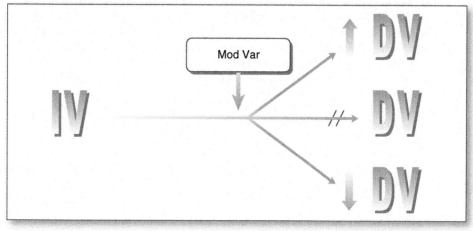

The relationship between the IV and DV is changed by another variable. The moderating variable may strengthen, weaken, or nullify the relationship between the IV and DV.
For example,

IV   Moderating variable   DV

Condom use   Age   STI

If the causal relationship between condom use and STIs is stronger in younger people, perhaps because they are having more sex with more partners, and weaker in older people, who tend to be in monogamous relationships, then age moderates the effect of condom use on STI incidence.

The relationship between the IV and DV is accounted for by another variable.
For example,

IV   Mediating variable   DV

Level of education   Condom use   STI

If highly educated people have fewer STIs than poorly educated people, then condom use might be a mediating variable. The relationship between level of education is explained by the greater use of condoms by better-educated people.

Mediating Variables

Sometimes the relationship between cause and effect is directly linked—your baseball strikes a window, and it breaks. However, there are many instances when this relationship is anything but direct—you look at a bright light, and your pupil constricts. Certainly, this is a cause-and-effect relationship, but there are many intervening steps. Suppose you just had an eye examination and the doctor used eye drops to dilate your pupils. What will this do to the cause-and-effect relationship? You leave the office and go into the bright sunlight and . . . nothing, no pupil constriction. Clearly, the eye drops are acting on some mediating variable between the light and the pupil constriction.

Identifying mediating variables may be centrally important to your research or entirely trivial depending on how the research fits into the particular theory. For much behavioral research, the mediating variables may be unimportant. Instead, the focus is on identifying and describing the environmental cues (cause) that elicit behavior (effect). Contrast this position with cognitive research, where much of the focus is on identifying mediating variables.

In the Knez (2001) study, the identification of a mediating variable was an important point. He was trying to show that the characteristics of light do not directly influence cognitive performance but, rather, that the light influences the participant's mood and that change in mood, in turn, affects the participant's performance.

In another example of a mediating variable, Lassri and Shahar (2012) examined whether childhood maltreatment affects the quality of romantic relationships between adults. They administered a questionnaire to 91 undergraduate students at the University of Negev, Israel, and measured a number of variables, including childhood emotional maltreatment, self-criticism, and quality of romantic relationships. By using a correlational technique called structural equation modeling (which will be discussed later in this chapter), they found that emotional maltreatment in childhood is related to increased incidence of self-criticism and that self-criticism is related to poor romantic relationships. In other words, a childhood of emotional maltreatment makes a person more likely to engage in critical self-statements, which leads to the person experiencing troubled romantic relationships as an adult. Self-criticism is a mediating variable between childhood emotional maltreatment and adult romantic relationships.

The introduction gives us a good understanding of the important variables in the study. In the method section, we will find detailed information about how the study was conducted and which measures were used.

The Method Section

Although the variables of the research are defined and discussed in the introduction, it is in the method section where you will read the details of exactly how these variables are measured, manipulated, or controlled. Indeed, if there is a theme to the method section, it would be details, details, details. You should find enough (dare we say it again) details in the method section to replicate the study on your own. That is, you should have all the necessary information to repeat the study as it was done by the authors, with different participants, of course.

The method section is typically divided into a number of subsections, usually separated with subheads (for more detail on writing a method section, see Chapter 14). The first subsection, typically called *Participants*, if human, and *Subjects*, if animal, will provide information about who or what was included in the research. You will read how the participants were recruited into the study or how the animals were obtained. Demographic information will be included, such as age, gender, race, and education level. If nonhuman subjects were used, details of care and housing will be described. Of course, you will also read how many participants were included.

You may find a subsection called *Materials* and/or *Apparatus*. Here, you will find manufacturers and model numbers of equipment and apparatus, details of tests and measures and the conditions of testing, and often a description of any stimulus materials used. Somewhere in the method section, you will read a description of the research design and the statistical tests. It does not necessarily make for good reading, but the purpose is to provide fine detail, not to entertain. It is in the method section that we find out exactly what was done. The procedure is described in a subsection called, well, *Procedure*. This is often written as a chronological sequence of what happened to the participants. Again, as with all the subsections of the method section, it is written in painstaking detail.

In our example article, Knez (2001) tells us he studied 54 women and 54 men, all 18 years old and all in high school. The basic design is described as a factorial between-subjects (his word, not ours) design (see Chapter 7) with three different lights and two genders. He also describes the testing conditions, details of the lighting (the IV), and the various dependent measures. He describes the procedure of the experiment, providing the time of day of testing, the information participants were given, and the order in which the tests were administered. At the end of the section, we have enough information that we could probably replicate the study exactly as he had done.

After reading the introduction and the method section, we now know quite a bit about the research area, the current researcher's study, and how he or she carried it out. It is time to find out what happened.

The Results

The results section is the part of the article that is the most exciting. This is where we learn whether or not the data support the research hypothesis. Typically, the section begins with a general statement addressing that very point (i.e., did the data support or fail to support the researcher's hypothesis?). As with the other sections, more detail on writing an article is presented in Chapter 14.

The results section is the most important section of a research article. Unfortunately, students can become overwhelmed by all the statistics. Even students who have done very well in their statistics courses can find the results sections of most research articles impossible to understand. The problem is that basic statistics courses cover *basic statistics* such as measures of central tendency (the mean, median, and mode) and measures of variability (the range, variance, and standard deviation). Of course, these statistics will appear in the results section and are widely used for describing and summarizing the data.

The problem is often in the *tests of significance*. Your basic statistics course probably covered the *z* test, *t* test, analysis of variance (ANOVA), and associated *F* test. You may have also learned about correlation and simple regression and, perhaps, chi-square tests. These are good statistics and are used sometimes in research, but unfortunately, when you go to read the literature, you will find statistical tests that you may have never heard of. We do not intend to teach advanced statistics here, but we do want to provide you with a conceptual understanding of these statistics so that when you read the literature you will have at least a basic understanding of these procedures. So, as briefly as we can, we are going to review statistics. No, you do not need a calculator; this review is at a conceptual level only, but in Chapter 13, we provide you with more of the nitty-gritty of basic statistics, which you may need to do a research project of your own.

In research, statistics are used for two purposes. The first is to *summarize* all the data and to make it simpler to talk about the outcome of research. These are typically called descriptive statistics. The second purpose is to *test research hypotheses*, and these are called inferential statistics.

Descriptive Statistics

Descriptive statistics include measures of central tendency, variability, and the strength of the relationship between variables. The mean, median, and mode are the most common measures of central tendency. The mean (symbolized as *M*) is the arithmetic average. It is what we report when talking about the class average on a test, for example. The median (symbolized as *Mdn*) is the value that half the observations (or scores) exceeded and half were below. It is the middle score in a distribution of scores arranged from lowest to highest. The median is often reported when a distribution of scores is not bell shaped (i.e., not a normal distribution). The mode (symbolized as *Mo*) is the most frequently occurring score or value in your data. The mode gives us a measure of the typical value in the distribution. For example, if you were making a "one-size-fits-all" pair of eyeglasses, you would want the mode for head size. Each measure of central tendency uses a different approach to describe the average of a group of scores.

The most common statistics used for describing variability in data are the range, variance, and standard deviation. The range either is reported as the highest and lowest score or is reduced to a single value that is the distance between these two scores. On an exam, you may ask what was the highest score attained, and perhaps out of morbid curiosity, you may want to know the lowest score as well. The range is an appropriate measure of variability for some types of data, but it is quite crude. For example, there may be one very high score and one very low score, and the range will not indicate that perhaps all the other scores were concentrated very near the mean. Two related measures of variability provide this information. The variance and its square root, the standard deviation (symbolized as *SD*), provide a measure of the average distance scores are from the mean. With data that are bell shaped or normally distributed, the standard deviation tells us where the bulk of the scores fall; about two thirds of the scores fall between 1 standard deviation above the mean and 1 standard deviation below the mean. More detail on the calculation and appropriate selection of these statistics is given in Chapters 5 and 13.

Often you will read research articles that describe the degree to which variables are related to one another. The most common measure of association is the Pearson product–moment correlation (symbolized as r). This statistic describes how strongly (or weakly) variables are related to one another. For example, if two variables are perfectly correlated, the r value will be 1 or −1. The sign of the number indicates the direction of the relationship. A positive correlation tells us that the variables are directly related; as one variable increases, so does the other, and as one variable decreases, so does the other. A negative correlation tells us that the variables are inversely related. That is, as one variable increases, the other decreases, and as one variable decreases, the other increases. The magnitude of r tells us how strongly the variables are related. A zero correlation tells us that the variables are not related at all; as the value increases to +1 or decreases to −1, the strength of the relationship increases. A correlation of 1 (either positive or negative) is called a perfect correlation. Be aware that perfect correlations never actually occur in the real world. If they do, it usually means that you have inadvertently measured the same variable twice and correlated the data. For example, you would likely get a correlation of 1 if you measured reaction time in seconds and also in minutes. It would be no surprise to find that the values are correlated because they are the same measure, only in different scales. Here is another example: Suppose you measured mood with two scales. It is likely that the measures will correlate highly. Again, this only indicates that you have two measures of the same thing.

These descriptive statistics are used to summarize what was observed in the research. But the idea of a lot of research is to generalize the findings beyond just the observations or participants in the study. We ultimately want to say something about behavior in general, not just the behavior that occurred in the study. To make these generalizations, we need inferential statistics. Before leaping into a list of the various inferential statistics you will likely come across in the literature, we would like to review some of the basic concepts of inference.

Inferential Statistics

Inferential statistics are used to generalize the findings of a study to a whole population. An *inference* is a general statement based on limited data. Statistics are used to attach a probability estimate to that statement. For example, a typical weather forecast does not tell you that it will rain tomorrow afternoon. Instead, the report will indicate the probability of rain tomorrow. Indeed, the forecast here for tomorrow is a 60% chance of rain. The problem with making an inference is that we might be wrong. No one can predict the future, but based on good meteorological information, an expert is able to estimate the probability of rain tomorrow. Similarly, in research, we cannot make generalized statements about everyone when we only include a sample of the population in our study. What we do instead is attach a probability estimate to our statements.

When you read the results of research articles, the two most common uses of inferential statistics will be hypothesis testing and confidence interval estimation.

- Does wearing earplugs improve test performance?
- Is exercise an effective treatment for depression?

- Is there a relationship between hours of sleep and ability to concentrate?
- Are married couples happier than single individuals?

These are all examples of research hypotheses that could be tested using inferential tests of significance. What about the following?

- Does the general public have confidence in its nation's leader?
- How many hours of sleep do most adults get?
- At what age do most people begin dating?

These are all examples of research with a focus on describing attitudes and/or behavior of a population. This type of research, which is more common in sociology than in psychology, uses confidence interval estimation instead of tests of significance.

The vast majority of psychological research involves testing a research hypothesis. So let's first look at the types of tests of significance you will likely see in the literature and then look at confidence intervals.

Common Tests of Significance. Results will be referred to as either statistically significant or not statistically significant. What does this mean? In hypothesis-testing research, a straw person argument is set up where we assume that a null hypothesis is true, and then we use the data to disprove the null and thus support our research hypothesis. Statistical significance means that it is unlikely that the null hypothesis is true given the data that were collected. Nowhere in the research article will you see a statement of the null hypothesis, but instead you will see statements about how the research hypothesis was supported or not supported. These statements will look like this:

- With an alpha of .01, those wearing earplugs performed statistically significantly better ($M = 35$, $SD = 1.32$) than those who were not ($M = 27$, $SD = 1.55$), $t(84) = 16.83$, $p = .002$.

- The small difference in happiness between married ($M = 231$, $SD = 9.34$) and single individuals ($M = 240$, $SD = 8.14$) was not statistically significant, $t(234) = 1.23$, $p = .21$.

These statements appear in the results section and describe the means and standard deviations of the groups and then a statistical test of significance (*t* test in both examples). In both statements, statistical significance is indicated by the italic *p*. This value is the *p* value. It is an estimate of the probability that the null hypothesis is true. Because the null hypothesis is the opposite of the research hypothesis, we want this value to be low. The accepted convention is a *p* value lower than .05 or, better still, lower than .01. The results will support the research hypothesis when the *p* value is lower than .05 or .01. The results will not support the research hypothesis when the *p* value is greater than .05. You may see a nonsignificant result reported as *ns* with no *p* value included.

You will find a refresher on statistical inference, including a discussion of Type I and Type II errors, and statistical power in Chapter 4.

Researchers using inferential techniques draw inferences based on the outcome of a statistical significance test. There are numerous tests of significance, each appropriate to a particular research question and the measures used, as you will recall from your introductory statistics course. It is beyond the scope of our book to describe in detail all or even most of these tests. You might want to refresh your memory by perusing your statistics text, which of course you have kept, haven't you? We offer a brief review of some of the most common tests of significance used by researchers in the "Basic Statistical Procedures" section.

Going back to the results section of our example article, we see that the author has divided that section into a number of subsections. The first section, with the heading "Mood," reports the effect of light on mood. It is only one sentence: "No significant results were obtained" (Knez, 2001, p. 204). The results section is typically brief, but the author could have provided the group means and the statistical tests that were not statistically significant. The next subsection, titled "Perceived Room Light Evaluation," provides a statistically significant effect. Knez (2001) reports a significant (meaning statistically significant) gender difference. He reports Wilks' lambda, which is a statistic used in multivariate ANOVA (MANOVA; when there is more than one DV), and the associated F statistic and p value for the gender difference, $F(7, 96) = 3.21, p = .04$. He also includes a figure showing the mean evaluations by men and women of the four light conditions and separate F statistics and p values for each condition.

In the subsections that follow, Knez (2001) reports the results and statistical tests for the effect of light condition on the various DVs. One of the effects he reports as a "weak tendency to a significant main effect" (p. 204) with a p value of .12. We would simply say that it was not statistically significant, *ns*. Indeed, many of his statistical tests produced p values greater than .05. We bring this to your attention as a reminder that even peer-reviewed journal articles need to be read with a critical eye. Don't just accept everything you read. You need to pay attention to the p values and question when they are not less than .05. You also need to examine the numbers carefully to discern the effect size.

What is noticeably missing from the results section of Knez (2001), our example article, is a calculation of effect size. *Effect size* gives us some indication of the strength of the effect (see Chapter 4 for more detail). Remember, statistical significance tells us that an effect was likely not due to chance and is probably a reliable effect. What statistical significance does not indicate is how large the effect is. If we inspect the numbers in Knez's article, we see that the effects were not very large. For example, on the short-term recall task, the best performance was from the participants in the warm-lighting conditions. They had a mean score of 6.9 compared with the other groups, with a mean score of about 6.25. A difference of only 0.65 of a word on a recall task seems like a pretty small effect, but then again, one would hardly expect that lighting conditions would have a dramatic effect on performance.

Once you have finished reading the introduction, method, and results sections, you should have a pretty good idea about what was done, to whom, and what was found. In the discussion section, you will read the researcher's interpretation of the research, comments about unexpected findings, and speculations about the importance of the work or its application.

The Discussion

The dissertation adviser of one of the authors of this book told her that he never read the discussion section of research reports. He was not interested in the interpretation of the authors. He interpreted the findings and their importance himself. We consider this good advice for seasoned researchers but not for students. The discussion section of a research article is where the author describes how the results fit into the literature. This is a discussion of the theories that are supported by the research and the theories that are not. It is also where you will find suggestions from the author as to where the research should go in the future—what questions are left unanswered and what new questions the research raises. Indeed, the discussion section may direct you in your selection of a research project. You may wish to contact the author to see if research is already being conducted on the questions posed in the discussion. Remember that it is important to be a critical consumer of research. Do not simply accept what is said in the discussion. Ask yourself if the results really do support the author's conclusions. Are there other possible interpretations?

In the discussion section of our example article, Knez (2001) relates the findings to his previous work and the research of others. He discusses the lack of effect of light on mood and questions the mood measure that was used. We think that another possibility, which he does not explore, is that lighting *may not have* an influence on mood. He also describes the effect of light on cognitive performance as being something new to the literature. We could speculate that this small effect might not be a reliable finding. Certainly, the weak p values reported in the results section would indicate either that the study should be replicated or that the results were a fluke. Again, as we said before, you need to be critical when reading the literature.

BASIC STATISTICAL PROCEDURES

Tests of Significance

t Test. The simplest experiment involves two groups, an experimental group and a control group. The researchers treat the groups differently (the IV) and measure their performance (the DV). The question then is "Did the treatment work?" Are the groups significantly different after receiving the treatment? If the research involves comparing means from two groups, the t test may be the appropriate test of significance. Be aware that the t test can also be used in nonexperimental studies. For example, a researcher who compares the mean performance of women with that of men might use a t test, but this is not an experiment.

Typically, a researcher will report the group means, whether the difference was statistically significant, and the t-test results. In essence, the t test is an evaluation of the difference between two means relative to the variability in the data. Simply reporting the group means is not enough because a large difference between two means might not be statistically significant when examined relative to the large variability of the scores of each group. Alternatively, a small difference between two means may be statistically significant if there is very little variation in scores within each group. The t test is a good test when you want to compare two groups, but what if you have more than two groups?

F Test. The *F* test of significance is used to compare means of more than two groups. There are numerous experimental (and quasi-experimental) designs, known as ANOVAs, that are analyzed with the *F* test. Indeed, when we were graduate students, we took entire courses in ANOVA. In general, the *F* test, like the *t* test, compares between-group variability with within-group variability.

As with the *t* test, the researcher will report the group means and whether the differences were statistically significant. From a significant *F* test, the researcher knows that at least two means were significantly different. To specify which groups were different from which others, the researcher must follow the *F* test with post hoc (after the fact) comparisons. For example, if there were three groups and the *F* test was statistically significant, a post hoc test might find that all three group means were statistically significantly different or perhaps that only one mean differed from the other two. There are a large number of post hoc tests (e.g., Scheffé, Tukey's least significant difference, and Bonferroni) that have slightly different applications. What is common to all these tests is that each produces a *p* value that is used to indicate which means differ from which.

As indicated above, many designs are analyzed with an *F* test, and they have names that indicate the number of IVs. You will find a one-way ANOVA used when there is one IV, a two-way ANOVA when there are two IVs, and a three-way ANOVA (you guessed it) when there are three. A null hypothesis is tested for each IV by calculating an *F* statistic. The advantage of the two- and three-way ANOVAs is that an interaction effect can also be tested. An interaction occurs when different combinations of the levels of the IVs have different effects on the DV. For example, if we wanted to investigate the effect of environmental noise (silent vs. noisy) on reading comprehension and the effect of different-colored paper (white, yellow, pink) on reading comprehension, we could use a two-way ANOVA to evaluate the effect of each IV and also whether the color of paper might interact with the noise to influence reading comprehension. It may be that noise produces a reduction in reading comprehension for white paper but not for yellow or pink paper. The interaction effect is important because it indicates that a variable is acting as a moderating variable. In this example, the effect of environmental noise on reading comprehension is moderated by the color of the paper.

There is another type of ANOVA that is used to control for a possible confounding variable. This procedure also uses the *F* statistic and is called analysis of covariance, or ANCOVA. Using our paper color example, suppose we want to test whether the color of paper will influence reading comprehension but our participants vary considerably in age. This could pose a serious confound because reading comprehension changes with age. If we measured age, we can use ANCOVA to remove variability in reading comprehension that is due to age and then test the effect of color. The procedure removes the variance due to age from the DV before the *F* is calculated for the effect of color. Consequently, we are testing the effect of color after we have taken into account the effect of age.

The statistics described above are useful for comparing group means, but you may come across research where the variables are categories and the data are summarized by counting the frequency of things. When there are frequency counts instead of scores, you may see a chi-square test.

Chi-Square Test. Do people prefer Coke or Pepsi? Suppose we have offered both drinks and asked people to declare a preference. We count the number of people preferring each drink. These data are not measures, and means cannot be calculated. If people's preference did not differ between the two drinks, we would expect about the same number of people to pick each, and we could use a chi-square test, called the goodness-of-fit test, to test our hypothesis. In chi-square, our null hypothesis is that our observed frequencies will not be different from those we would expect by chance.

In the literature, you will likely see the data summarized by reporting the frequencies of each category either as total counts or perhaps as percentages of the total. Then, you may read a statement that the frequencies in the groups are statistically significant, followed by a report of the chi-square statistic and *p* value.

Chi-square is called a *nonparametric* or *distribution-free* test because the test does not make the assumption that the population is distributed normally. Indeed, hypotheses about the *shape* of the population distribution are exactly what we are testing with chi-square.

There are two common chi-square tests: the goodness-of-fit test and the test for independence. The goodness-of-fit test is used when there are categorical data on one variable, as we had in the soft drink preference example. Perhaps a researcher is interested in the relationship between two categorical variables. In this case, you might see the chi-square test for independence. Imagine our researcher has asked cola tasters to indicate their choice of cola and has also categorized them by age. The research hypothesis might be that preference for cola depends on age. The researcher might think that younger people prefer Pepsi, for example, and older people prefer Coke. Or perhaps older people have no preference. The chi-square statistic is the same for this test as for the goodness-of-fit test. The difference is in the hypothesis. The null is that the two variables are independent (i.e., there is no relationship between them). In a research article, you will likely see a table of frequencies (or percentages), a statement as to whether a relationship was found between the variables, and the chi-square statistic and *p* value.

CONCEPTUAL EXERCISE 2B

For each of the following, decide if a *t* test, an *F* test, or a chi-square test might be appropriate:

1. A new teacher decides to put some of the principles he learned in school to the test. He randomly selects half of his class and consistently praises each student for being on the task for a minimum period of time. With the other half of the class, he periodically gives praise for on-task behavior. He wants to know if periodic praise produces more on-task behavior than consistent praise.

2. Psychiatric walk-in clients are randomly assigned to five therapists for short-term counseling. One therapist specializes in psychoanalytic techniques, one in client-centered techniques, one in behavioral techniques, and one in cognitive techniques. The fifth therapist is eclectic, using techniques from each of the above therapies. All clients are rated on various scales designed to measure improvement. Mean improvement ratings of the clients for each therapist are compared.

3. A statistics professor wants to know if generally there are more or less equal numbers of psychology, sociology, and business students. She keeps a tally.

Other Nonparametric Tests. In addition to chi-square, there are numerous other nonparametric tests that you will see in the literature. We have not tried to present a complete list here, but instead we have included the more common tests.

A nonparametric alternative to a *t* test for independent groups is the *Mann-Whitney U test*, which detects differences in central tendency and differences in the entire distributions of rank-ordered data. The *Wilcoxon signed-ranks test* is an alternative to a *t* test for dependent groups for rank-order data on the same or matched participants.

A nonparametric alternative to the one-way ANOVA is the *Kruskal–Wallis H test*, used when the data are rank orders of three or more independent groups. When those groups are dependent (i.e., repeated measures), a nonparametric test is the Friedman test.

Pearson's r Test. If you earned a lot of money, would you be happy? Is there a relationship between income and happiness? If a researcher were interested in investigating a linear relationship between two continuous variables, he or she would use the Pearson product–moment test to calculate the correlation *r.* If you are getting a sense of déjà vu, it is probably because we talked about *r* as a descriptive statistic, but here, we are talking about it as an inferential statistic. The important distinction is that the *r* reported as an inferential statistic will have an associated *p* value. For example, in a research article, you will read that a positive relationship was found between a measure of need for achievement and years of education and that the relationship was statistically significant. If the relationship was statistically significant, then you will also see a *p* value reported.

Regression. Regression is related to correlation, but in regression, we are interested in using a predictor variable to predict a criterion variable. Continuing with the example of need for achievement and education, perhaps the researcher was also interested in predicting need for achievement from education level. If the correlation between the two variables is statistically significant, then it is a simple matter of fitting a line through the data and using the equation for the line to predict need for achievement from education level. We say simple matter because the calculations are all done by computer, but certainly, the equation for a straight line is simple:

$$Y = mX + b$$

where *Y* is the criterion variable, *X* is the predictor variable, *m* is the slope of the line, and *b* is the value of *Y* where the line intercepts the *y*-axis. Be sure to keep in mind as you read the research that the accuracy of the predicted values will be as good as the correlation is. That is, the closer the correlation is to $+1$ (or -1), the better the predictions will be.

The statistical procedures we have been discussing all involve an a priori hypothesis about the nature of the population. Hypothesis testing is used a lot in psychology. Some other disciplines tend to prefer post hoc procedures, and you will find confidence interval estimates quite often in the literature you will be reading.

Confidence Intervals

Confidence intervals are used when we are interested in estimating population parameters. We are still making an inference from a sample to a population, and because of that, we are using probability estimates. But instead of reporting a *p* value indicating the probability that the null is true, we report the probability that our estimate about the population is true. Pollsters describing political candidates often use confidence intervals. For example, you may have read reports that, based on a poll of 1,000 respondents, 83% say they would vote for *X* if there were an election tomorrow. These statements are typically followed with a statement such as "These results are accurate to within 3 percentage points 19 times out of 20." What does this mean? It means that, based on a sample of 1,000, the population support for the candidate is probably somewhere between 83% − 3% and 83% + 3% or somewhere between 80% and 86%. Are they absolutely sure? No, they say the estimate should be correct 19 times out of 20 or 95% of the time (19/20 = .95). So a *p* value of .05 from hypothesis testing becomes a confidence interval of .95, and similarly, a *p* value of .01 becomes a confidence interval of.99 (reported as 99 times out of 100). Again, in hypothesis testing, we report a significance test with a *p* value that indicates the probability that the null is true. In confidence intervals, we report an interval within which we estimate the true population parameter to fall.

Important note to students:

If you're reading this material and starting to get anxious, relax! Our intention here is to discuss these inferential statistics at a conceptual level. As we indicated earlier, when you begin reading the literature, it is unlikely that you will see research using *t* tests or simple ANOVAs. What you will see are complex statistics that may be completely new to you. Our intention here is to give you enough information to understand what is being described in the literature.

MORE COMPLEX STATISTICAL PROCEDURES

Multiple Regression. If predicting someone's performance using one predictor variable is a good idea, then using more than one predictor variable is a better idea. Entire textbooks are devoted to multiple regression techniques, but the basic idea is to use more than one predictor variable, X_1, X_2, X_3, and so on, to predict one criterion variable, *Y*. As with simple regression, multiple regression requires the fitting of a line through your data, but first, all the predictor variables are combined, and then the linear combination of *X*s is correlated with *Y*. It is easy to visualize multiple regression with two predictors. This would be a line in dimensional space. Imagining more than two predictors is difficult and fortunately not necessary. Multiple regression produces an *r* value that reflects how well the linear combination of *X*s predicts *Y*. Some predictor variables are likely to be better predictors of *Y* than others, and the analysis produces weights that can be used in a regression equation to predict *Y*. Simply multiply the values of the predictor variables by their respective weights, and you have your predicted value.

$$Y(\text{predicted}) = B_1(X_1) + B_2(X_2) + B_3(X_3) + \ldots + \text{Constant}$$

In addition to the weights used to predict criterion values, multiple regression analysis also provides standardized weights called *beta* (β) *weights*. These values tell us something about each individual predictor in the regression analysis. They can be interpreted much like an *r* value, with the sign indicating the relationship between the predictor variable and the criterion variable and the magnitude indicating the relative importance of the variable in predicting the criterion. Thus, in a multiple regression analysis, we can examine the relative contribution of each predictor variable in the overall analysis.

As you just learned, multiple regression is used to determine the influence of several predictor variables on a single criterion variable. Let's look briefly at two useful concepts in multiple regression: (1) partial and (2) semipartial (also called part) correlation.

Partial Correlation. Sometimes we would like to measure the relationship between two variables when a third has an influence on them both. We can partial out the effects of that third variable by computing a partial correlation. Suppose there is a correlation between age and income. It seems reasonable that older people might make more money than younger people. Is there another variable that you think might be related to age and income? How about years of education? Older people are more likely to be better educated, having had more years to go to school, and it seems likely that better-educated people earn more. So what is the true relationship between age and income if the variable *years of education* is taken out of the equation? One solution would be to group people by years of education and then conduct a number of separate correlations between age and income for each education group. Partial correlation, however, provides a better solution by telling us what the true relationship is between age and income when years of education has been partialled out.

Semipartial Correlation. As we just discussed, in partial correlation, we remove the relationship of one variable from the other variables and then calculate the correlation. But what if we want to remove the influence of a variable from *only one* of the other variables? This is called a semipartial correlation. For example, at our school, we accept senior students in our applied psychology program based on their grades in the first and second years. We have found a strong positive correlation between previous grades and performance in our program. Suppose we could also administer an entrance exam to use as another predictor but the exam was expensive. We can use semipartial correlation to determine how much the entrance test will increase our predictive power over and above using previous grades.

How do we do this? Well, we correlate entrance test scores and performance in the program after first removing the influence of previous grades on program performance. This correlation value then will tell us what relationship remains between entrance test scores and program performance when the correlation with previous grades has been partialled out of program performance but not out of entrance test scores. In our example, we could decide, based on this correlation, whether an expensive entrance test helped our predictive ability enough for us to go ahead and use it.

Logistic Regression. Suppose you were interested in predicting whether a young offender would reoffend. You measure a number of possible predictor variables, such as degree of social support, integration in the community, job history, and so on, and then follow your participants for 5 years and measure if they reoffend. The predictor variables may be continuous, but the criterion variable is discrete; they reoffend or they don't. When we have a discrete criterion variable, we use logistic regression. Just as we used a combination of the predictor variables to predict the criterion variable in multiple regression, we do the same thing in logistic regression. The difference is that instead of predicting a value for the criterion variable, we predict the likelihood of the occurrence of the criterion variable. We express this as an *odds ratio*—that is, the odds of reoffending divided by the odds of not reoffending. If the probability of reoffending is .75 (i.e., there is a 75% chance of reoffending), then the probability of not reoffending is .25 (1 − .75). The odds of reoffending are .75/.25, or 3:1, and the odds of not reoffending are .25/.75, or .33. We calculate the odds ratio of reoffending versus not reoffending as .75/.33, or 2.25. In other words, the odds of reoffending are two and a quarter times higher than those of not reoffending.

Factor Analysis. Factor analysis is a correlational technique we use to find simpler patterns of relationships among many variables. Factor analysis can tell us if a large number of variables can be explained by a much smaller number of uncorrelated constructs or factors.

In psychology, one of the best examples of factor analysis is in the area of personality theory. What psychology student hasn't heard of OCEAN? These five personality factors of Openness, Conscientiousness, Extraversion, Agreeableness, and Neuroticism were described by McCrae and Costa (1987) as the only factors needed to describe someone's personality. Though we may use hundreds of traits and characteristics to describe someone's personality, these all factor down to just five unique dimensions. This factoring down was accomplished by factor analysis.

In factor analysis, the researcher is looking for underlying and independent factors that *have not* been directly measured to explain a lot of variables that *have* been measured. The procedure involves identifying the variables that are interrelated. Once the factors have been identified, it is up to the researcher to decide what construct this group of variables is measuring. These underlying factors are hypothetical—that is, inferred by the researcher. The researcher attempts to find the smallest number of factors that can adequately explain the observed variables and to determine the fundamental nature of those factors.

When you read a research report where factor analysis has been used, you will probably see a complicated-looking matrix called a correlation matrix. Don't be discouraged. Keep in mind that although the mathematics are complex and beyond the scope of this book, the concept is reasonably simple. Can an underlying variable such as general intelligence explain a whole lot of variation in measures of mental abilities?

Cluster Analysis. Cluster analysis includes a range of algorithms and methods used to group similar objects into categories, or clusters. The members of each cluster are thus more similar to each other than they are to members of other clusters. Unlike factor analysis, where the goal is to group similar variables together, in cluster analysis, the idea is to group similar members. Organizing data into meaningful structures or *taxonomies* is a task many researchers face. Cluster analysis is a method that can discover structure in data, but it does not in and of itself have any explanatory function. In other words, the analysis can find structure but does not explain it.

Imagine a hospital where patients are assigned to wards based on similar symptoms or perhaps similar treatments. Each ward could be considered a cluster. A cluster analysis might discover the similarities among the patients in each ward, and the researcher then has the job of determining why the cluster or ward is similar (i.e., symptoms, treatment, age, etc.).

Cluster analysis is often used when researchers have no a priori hypotheses and are in the beginning phase of their research. As such, statistical significance testing often has no role in such analyses.

Structural Equation Modeling. Structural equation modeling is a complex endeavor that can involve various techniques, including factor analysis, regression models, path analysis, and so on. We will just be able to give you an idea of the purpose of structural equation modeling here.

We hope you will remember what happens when we transform a set of numbers by adding a constant to each or multiplying each by a constant. Let's say we multiply all the numbers in a list by a constant c. The mean of that set of transformed numbers will be equal to the old mean times c, the standard deviation of the new set of numbers will equal the old standard deviation times the absolute value (i.e., ignore the sign) of c, and the variance will equal the old variance times c squared. Simple, right?

What is our point, you might be wondering? Well, bear with us. If we suspected that two sets of numbers were related, we could compare the variances of the two sets of numbers, for example, to confirm our suspicions. If one set was related to the other set by the equation $Y = 2X$, then the variance of Y must be four times the variance of X. So we could confirm our hypothesis about the relationship between the two sets of numbers by comparing their variances rather than the numbers themselves. We hope you are not too confused by this somewhat odd way of doing things, but we think it might help you understand structural equation modeling. Two sets of numbers could be related in much more mathematically complex ways than by $Y = 2X$, but we hope you are getting the idea. You can determine if variables are related by looking at their variances and covariances.

Structural modeling is a way of determining whether a set of variances and covariances fits a specific structural model. In essence, the researcher hypothesizes that the variables are related in a particular way, often with something called a *path diagram* that shows the interrelationships. Then, the researcher figures out what this model predicts about the values of the variances and covariances of the variables. This is the really complex part of the process, and we just can't go there! Then, the researcher examines the variances and covariances of the variables to see if they fit the predictions of the model.

As we said earlier, this is a complex procedure well beyond the scope of our book, but we hope our brief discussion gives you some idea of the purpose of structural equation modeling.

Discriminant Function Analysis. As we mentioned earlier, at our school, we offer an applied psychology degree program. One of our objectives is to prepare students for graduate work in applied areas. Imagine that we classified our graduates over the past 10 years into two groups: (1) students who were accepted into graduate school and (2) students who were not. We could use discriminant function analysis to predict acceptance into graduate school using grade point average and workshop attendance, for example. Our analysis might help us determine how grade point average and workshop attendance individually predict acceptance into graduate school and how a combination of both predicts acceptance.

This is the idea behind discriminant function analysis. Of course, we might have many more variables, and the analysis allows us to determine the predictive ability of each variable alone and in combination with other variables. If discriminant function analysis sounds like logistic regression, it is because they are related. They have similar applications, but discriminant function analysis is calculated as ANOVA with more than one DV (MANOVA). The various DVs are used to predict group membership.

This analysis, like the others discussed in this section, is much more complex than this, but again, we hope our brief discussion gives you an inkling about the use of these techniques so that when you read the literature, you will have some understanding about the research outcomes.

We hope that this chapter has prepared you, on a conceptual level, to understand the literature you will be reading as you continue with your social science studies. We now turn to a topic that is so important in social science research that we have devoted an entire chapter to it: research ethics.

CHAPTER SUMMARY

Once a general research topic has been selected, a *literature search* is necessary to determine what research has already been conducted in the area. Various databases are available for the psychology literature. One of the most useful is PsycINFO. Review articles, books, chapters in books, edited volumes, and chapters in edited volumes are also found in the research databases. Peer-reviewed journals are the best sources of original research. Searching the literature for relevant research will be more successful if appropriate *search terms* are used.

Original research journal articles generally include an *abstract*, an *introduction*, a *method* section, a *results* section, and a *discussion* section. The purpose of the abstract is to summarize the article. There should be enough information in the abstract for the reader to decide if he or she should read the entire research article. In the introduction, there will be a description of the *relevant research* and a description of the specific research hypotheses of the author(s). The IV and DVs are often described in the introduction, as well.

The method section is typically divided into subsections such as *Participants* or *Subjects*, *Materials*, and *Apparatus*. The method section always contains a subsection called *Procedure*. Enough details of the procedure must be included so that researchers elsewhere could replicate the research.

In the results section, the statistical data are presented. Both *descriptive* and *inferential statistics* will be reported. Descriptive measures of *central tendency*, *variability*, and the strength of the relationship between variables will be reported. Typically, the inferential statistics follow the descriptive statistics. A lot of psychology research involves testing hypotheses. Any *tests of significance* that were used to assess the research hypotheses will be reported in the results section. Basic tests of significance include *t tests*, *F tests*, *chi-square tests*, *correlation* and *regression* tests, and so on. The authors will indicate whether or not the hypotheses they put forth in the introduction were supported by the statistical analyses.

More complex analyses that are common in the research literature include *multiple regression*, *partial correlation*, *semipartial correlation*, *logistic regression*, *factor analysis*, *cluster analysis*, *structural equation modeling*, and *discriminant function analysis*.

Although hypothesis testing is more common in psychology research, *confidence interval* estimation is also used. A *confidence interval* is a range of values with a known probability of containing a parameter.

The discussion section of a research article contains the authors' interpretation of the statistical findings and suggestions about future research directions.

CHAPTER RESOURCES

ANSWERS TO CONCEPTUAL EXERCISES

Conceptual Exercise 2A

1a. IV is amount of practice; DV is reaction time.

1b. IV is amount of exercise; DV is ratings of depression.

Conceptual Exercise 2B

1. Because there are two groups, a *t* test might be appropriate.

2. There are five groups, and so an *F* test might be appropriate.

3. A chi-square goodness of fit test would answer this question.

FAQ

Q1: What's a DV dependent on?

A1: We hope it is dependent on our manipulation (the IV).

Q2: I have taken an intro stats course, and I can't make head or tail out of the research I am reading.

A2: We understand. The statistics used by most researchers today go well beyond what you learned in your intro stats course. You will need a graduate-level course under your belt to understand a lot of the statistics you will read about, but we hope you will be able to understand on a conceptual level a lot of what you read.

Q3: I just read a research article, and they talked about a bunch of correlation stuff and validity and reliability. I have no clue.

A3: Read Chapters 4 and 5.

Q4: I just read a paper that talked about stratified sampling.

A4: Go to Chapter 6.

Q5: My prof tells me to use APA style in my report, but the articles I have read don't look anything like the APA manual.

A5: Yes, each specific journal uses its own style. Go to Chapter 14.

CHAPTER EXERCISES

1. Identify the IV and DV for each of the following. Indicate any participant variables being examined.
   a. Does the use of imagery enhance athletic performance?
   b. Are teens more concerned about their bodies than older adults?
   c. Does repetition in advertising improve sales?
   d. Does straight alley training improve the speed of rats in a maze?
   e. Is there a difference in leadership style between men and women?

2. Why are peer-reviewed journals preferable? What does the term *blind review* mean?

3. List two things found in the introduction of a research article.

4. List and describe what is found in typical subsections of the method section of a research article.

5. List two kinds of statistics always found in the results section of a research article.

6. What is the purpose of the discussion section of a research article?

7. Describe the difference between a mediating and a moderating variable.

8. What is the general purpose of a significance test?

9. What is the general purpose of confidence interval estimation?

CHAPTER PROJECTS

1. Locate three research articles from peer-reviewed journals. Briefly summarize each article, and describe the IV (or participant/subject variables), DV, control procedures employed (and why they were needed), and descriptive statistics used. Discuss other ways by which the variables could have been operationalized.

2. With a search term of your choice, find three empirical research articles. Describe the methods the researchers used to increase the power of their analysis. Can you think of other ways to increase power in each study?

ANCILLARIES

Visit the companion website at www.sagepub.com/evans3e for these additional learning resources:

- Self-quizzes
- SAGE Journal Articles
- Video and Audio Links
- Additional Web Resources

Hypothesis Development: Where Research Questions Come From

McBride, D. M.

Consider the following questions as you read Chapter 2

- How do researchers develop a research question?
- How do researchers conduct a literature review?
- What are some useful resources for a literature review?
- What will you find in a literature review?
- What are the different types of research articles, and how are they organized?
- How do we use a literature review to make hypotheses?
- What are the different types of hypotheses that a researcher can make?

A few years ago, I was playing the game Catchphrase with some friends. In this game, a handheld device displays a target phrase (e.g., a name or object) while ticking down a timer. The players with the device must provide clues to the target phrase (without saying it) to get their teammates to say the phrase. Meanwhile, the timer ticks faster and faster until it runs out and buzzes. When the time runs out, the player who ends up with the device loses a point for their team. The game moves swiftly, with teammates constantly calling out phrases to guess the target phrase.

After the game ended, we discussed the sequence of guessing of a particularly difficult phrase. Two players, Joel and Renée, claimed to have guessed the phrase, but only one had actually done so. Everyone agreed that Renée had actually guessed the phrase, but Joel claimed to have a clear memory of guessing it. It was determined that although Joel believed that he had guessed the correct phrase, he actually did not accurately recall (had an inaccurate memory) the events of the game. He had a *false memory* in remembering who had actually guessed correctly. Perplexed by his error, Joel suggested that "someone should study this." As a memory researcher, I became interested in this phenomenon and conducted experiments to investigate false memories like the one that Joel had during the game (e.g., Coane & McBride, 2006; McBride, Coane, & Raulerson, 2006). This story illustrates how everyday events such as these can spark psychological research questions (e.g., Why do false memories occur?).

DEVELOPING A RESEARCH QUESTION

Choosing a research question is the first step in the research process (see Figure 2.1). Answering a research question is the researcher's primary motivation for designing and conducting a study. These questions come from many sources. Primarily, they come from what the researcher is interested in learning about. Think about what topics in psychology interest you the most. Can you think of questions about behavior that you would like to have answered? Have you ever asked yourself a "What if . . . " question about a behavior? That is often where research questions begin—from the questions a researcher is interested in. In the situation described above, a research question was sparked by an everyday event (e.g., Why do false memories occur?). In other cases, research questions are developed to solve a real-world problem (e.g., How does the use of a cellular phone affect driving performance?). Finally, explanations of behavior that need to be tested (theories) can guide research questions (e.g., Do negative thoughts cause depression?).

Theory: an explanation of behavior that can be tested through research studies

Descriptive Research Question: a research question that asks about the presence of behavior, how frequently it is exhibited, or whether there is a relationship between different behaviors

Causal Research Question: a research question that asks what causes specific behaviors to occur

Research questions can be descriptive, such as whether a specific behavior occurs (Are college students anxious?), what the nature of the behavior is (How does anxiety manifest itself in college students?), or whether behaviors occur together (Do college students who smoke also tend to be anxious?). Questions can also be causal—about causes of behavior (What types of events cause college students to become anxious?). Many causal research questions are also designed to test a theory about the cause of a behavior (Is anxiety in college students caused by a lack of confidence in their abilities?) or to compare theories about behavior to see which theory has more support (Is anxiety in college students caused by a lack of confidence in their abilities or a lack of social support?). As described in Chapter 1, research questions can answer fundamental questions about behavior (What are the causes of anxiety among college students?) or questions about how to solve real-world problems (What kinds of student-oriented programs can a college or university initiate that will reduce anxiety in college students?). This is the difference between basic research questions and applied research questions. The type of question a researcher pursues is based on whether the researcher is interested in basic questions about a behavior or applications of the behavior in daily life. However, even though researcher interest is often a starting place for choosing a question to study, researchers should consider how appropriate their question is for both scientific methods and the specific field of study before moving on to designing a study.

One important issue in choosing a research question is whether the question can be answered with the scientific methods described in Chapter 1. Can observations of behavior provide an answer to the question? Some questions that would be difficult to test with

Figure 2.1   Steps in the Research Process: Choosing a Research Question

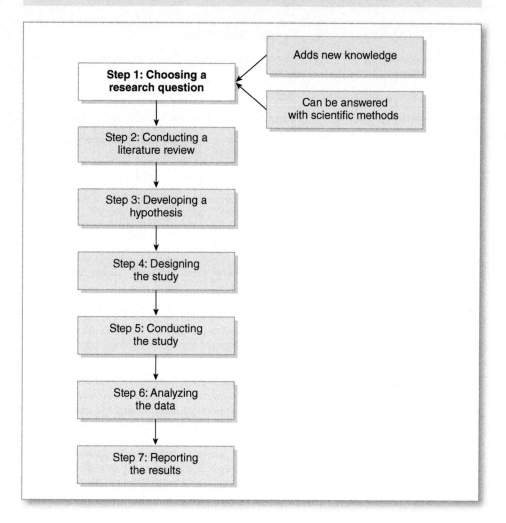

scientific methods are "Does God exist?" and "Was the Iraq War a moral war?" If specific observations of behavior can be made to help answer the question, then it might be an appropriate question for psychological research. Table 2.1 provides some examples of research questions that have been examined in different areas of psychological research to give you some examples of questions that can be answered by observing behavior. In addition, Chapter 4 describes some specific ways to observe behaviors and how they help answer a research question.

Another important consideration in choosing a research question is how much is already known about the question. In other words, what has been learned from previous studies about

Table 2.1 Examples of Research Questions in Different Areas of Psychology

Area of Psychological Research	Examples of Research Questions
Social psychology	How does an authority figure influence behavior? (Milgram, 1963)
	What types of faces are considered attractive? (Corneille, Monin, & Pleyers, 2005)
Cognitive psychology	What types of memory decline as people age? (Lipman & Caplan, 1992)
	How does our knowledge of the world influence our perception? (Ban, Lee, & Yang, 2004)
Industrial-organizational psychology	How does work environment affect job stress? (Pal & Saksvik, 2008)
	How does perception of power in the workplace affect perceptions of sexual harassment? (DeSouza & Fansler, 2003)
Clinical psychology	What types of people benefit most from cognitive behavioral therapy? (Green, Hadjistavropoulos, & Sharpe, 2008)
	What are the causes of schizophrenia? (Compton, Goulding, & Walker, 2007)
Biological psychology	What are the effects of amphetamine on the brain? (Heidenreich, 1993)
	What are the neurological causes of Parkinson's disease? (Olzmann, 2007)

the question? To investigate what is known about a research question from previous studies, a thorough literature review should be conducted. A literature review involves searching research databases or other sources to find relevant research that has been done in an area of the field. By reading about what other researchers have done, the literature review helps a researcher to determine what is already known about a research question, determine what methods have been used to investigate the question, and find information that can help him or her make a prediction about what the answer to the research question will be. (Making predictions will be discussed in detail later.) Conducting a literature review ensures that a new study will add to the knowledge in an area without duplicating what is already known. However, it can take many studies with the same research question before the answer to the research question is supported by enough evidence to allow for confidence in the answer. Thus, replication of results is an important part of the scientific process. Just because a study had been done before on a specific research question does not mean more studies are not needed to fully answer the question. A research question does not need to be wholly original to contribute to psychological science (Figure 2.2).

Literature Review: a process of searching for and reviewing previous studies related to a study being developed to add to the knowledge in an area and make appropriate predictions about the data

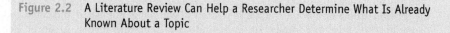

Figure 2.2 A Literature Review Can Help a Researcher Determine What Is Already Known About a Topic

SOURCE: Copyright by S. Harris, http://www.sciencecartoonsplus.com/scimags.html.

Stop and Think

(2.1) For each of the research questions below, identify whether they are descriptive or causal questions:

- How often does operant conditioning occur in daily life?
- Does jet lag affect one's mood?
- Can cognitive training decrease dementia?

(2.2) Explain why a researcher should conduct a literature review before conducting a study.

HOW TO CONDUCT A LITERATURE REVIEW

There are many sources researchers use to conduct a literature review. Searching through databases helps identify studies relevant to a research question. Databases may also hold references to helpful reviews of research in an area. However, if you want to learn about the most recent studies in an area, databases may not be the best source because these databases typically reference published works, and the publication process can take a year or more from the time an article or a book chapter is written to when it is published and cataloged in the database. Therefore, to conduct the most up-to-date literature review, it can be helpful to attend a psychological conference in an area where researchers often present studies that have not yet been published. More information about the sources for conducting a literature review is provided in the rest of this chapter (Figure 2.3).

PsycINFO

A very useful database for a literature review of psychological research is PsycINFO. PsycINFO is a searchable database that contains records of articles, books, and book chapters written by researchers about research studies in an area of psychology. Although each version may have a

Figure 2.3   Steps in the Research Process: Conducting a Literature Review

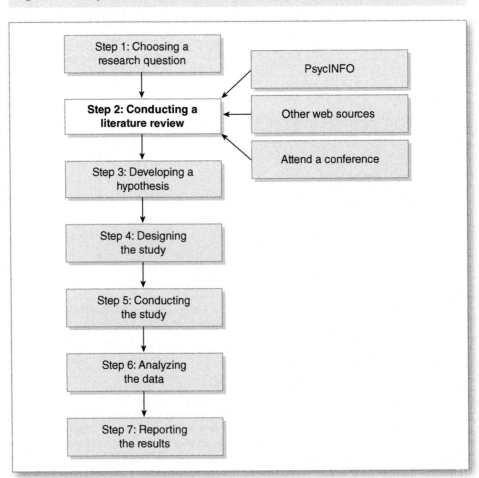

different appearance, all versions of PsycINFO can be searched by topic words, words that appear in the citation information for the article (this includes the title, authors, abstract, and topic words), author names, journal in which the article was published, and so on. In other words, there are many ways to find articles and book chapters about a research question using PsycINFO. Searching by topic words (called key words in PsycINFO) is a good way to start a search for a literature review.

There are two primary ways to search for articles and chapters by key words. One is to map the term to a subject heading. The American Psychological Association (APA) has designated specific subject headings as general topics of study in psychology. Each article or chapter has been coded by the subject headings that best describe the topic of the article. In PsycINFO, you click a box or a button to turn on the mapping to subject headings, and various subject headings appear that correspond to the key words you have typed in (you do not have to know the exact subject heading—PsycINFO searches for subject headings similar to what you type in). You can choose to focus on a specific heading or "auto explode" the search to include all the subheadings that might be contained in the more general heading. You can also choose to search just the key words you entered, which allows PsycINFO to search for articles and chapters that contain those words in the title or abstract. You can also combine searches that focus on different key words.

An example helps explain how this works (you can follow along by trying this out in PsycINFO if it is available at your college or university—if you have a different database available to you, such as PsycARTICLES, you may be able to follow this process, as most databases allow you to search in similar ways—see also http://www.apa.org/pubs/databases/training/search-guides.aspx for information on searching different databases). Suppose that you are interested in conducting a literature search for the relationship between depression and bullying behaviors in children. A good place to start is a key word search in PsycINFO. You can start by typing *depression* into the key word window and mapping it onto the subject headings if such an option is shown. A window such as the one shown in Table 2.2 may appear where you see several different forms of depression listed as well as the general heading of depression. Different versions of PsycINFO have different appearances, so your version may not show the window as it appears in Table 2.2, or it may display different subject terms. Continue to execute a search of articles that have *depression* anywhere in the full reference of the article (e.g., title, abstract, topic words). You should find that PsycINFO yields a large number of records that fit these key words. Depending on which subject terms you choose, different sets of articles are found. Obviously, there are far too many for us to search through one by one, so we need to narrow the search further and include the bullying portion of our topic.

We can conduct a second key word search for *bullying* using the same search procedure described above for depression. This search should find a large number of records as well but fewer records than the search for *depression* as there have been fewer studies conducted on the topic of bullying. Finally, to narrow our search to the specific topic we started with (depression and bullying), we can combine our two searches. Your version of PsycINFO may have a Combine function for this purpose. If not, you can type "1 and 2" into the search window and PsycINFO will combine the searches for you. If you combine your searches, you should find a more reasonable number of records to look at (when I conducted this search in June 2011, I found 192 records, but you may find more if your search terms include more choices or if additional articles have been published on these topics since that time).

Before we look at the results of the search, consider a possible outcome of our *bullying* search. Suppose that *bullying* was not the proper term, and we find no subject headings that

Table 2.2 An Example of a Key Word Search in PsycINFO for *Depression*: Each Version of PsycINFO May Have a Different Appearance

Select	Subject Heading	Auto Explode	Focus
O	Anaclitic depression	O	O
O	Atypical depression	O	O
O	Beck Depression Inventory (BDI)	O	O
O	"Depression (emotion)"	O	O
O	Endogenous depression	O	O
O	Major depression	O	O
	. . .		
O	depression.mp search as key word		

are relevant. One thing we can do to be certain that we get the right subject headings is to use a shorter form of our term and search for truncations. We can do this by shortening our term to *bully* and adding a "*" or "$" to the end of it in the search window. This addition searches for all words that begin with bully and finds any variations that might get us closer to our search objective. Be sure to use the truncation symbols if you are not certain that you have the right term or if you do not find appropriate subject headings with a given search term.

What will the PsycINFO search give you? If you view the results of the search we conducted above, you will see a list of articles (probably the most recently published articles first) that indicates the names of the authors, the title of the article, the type of article (journal article, book chapter, dissertation, etc.), and where and when the article was published. For each article, you can choose to view the *abstract* of the article. The abstract is a short paragraph that summarizes the content of the article (abstracts are discussed in detail later when the structure of journal articles is presented). You can then read through the abstracts of articles that might be relevant to your topic. You might also see a link to the article available online in PDF format or a link to search your library for the journal or book in which the article was published to assist you in locating any articles you find relevant to your literature review. Finally, the reference sections of the articles you find may also lead you to other relevant articles on your topic.

Suppose that you find an article that is especially relevant to your topic and that you would like to know if the same author has published other articles relevant to your topic. You can find articles by a particular author by conducting an author search in PsycINFO (you could also just click on the reference for the article and the author name will appear as a link that will give you a list of all articles in the database by that author). Simply type the author's last name and first initial into PsycINFO and you will see choices, in alphabetical order, that match what you typed. You can choose any that seem relevant (sometimes the same author will be listed in a few different ways—with or without middle initial) and PsycINFO will list the publications by that author. You can also limit key word and author searches by year if you are just interested in the most recent articles that have been published. Finally, articles in a particular psychology journal can be searched in PsycINFO (see below for a description of psychology journals). For more information on PsycINFO searches go to http://www.apa.org/pubs/databases/training/search-guides.aspx for APA guides on how to use PsycINFO.

PubMed and ERIC

Although most articles published in psychology journals can be found in PsycINFO or similar databases, some journals publish articles in other topic areas that overlap with psychology, and you will find them only in other databases. For example, journals that publish research in biological and medical areas can be found by searching the PubMed database. If you are interested in conducting a literature review on topics in biological psychology or about psychological disorders or specific conditions such as autism, you may want to search PubMed in addition to PsycINFO to complete a thorough literature review. Articles in areas related to education can be found in the ERIC (Education Resources Information Center) database. Thus, if you are conducting a literature review on topics such as standardized testing, you may also want to search for articles in ERIC. Like PsycINFO, PubMed and ERIC can be searched by topic, author, and journal with advanced search capabilities that can include year of publication, language of publication, and so on. The search screen will have a different layout, depending on the version of the database that you are viewing, but many versions of both PubMed and ERIC have drop-down menus for choosing a search by these features of an article. A database dealing with more general topics, called Web of Science, is also available for searching for journal articles in different areas of research.

Other Sources

In addition to PsycINFO and similar databases, there are search engines that can be accessed to obtain articles relevant to your topic. The first is a subengine of Google called *Google Scholar*. You can access Google Scholar at http://scholar.google.com/. Google Scholar searches the web for academic journals and books to find articles relevant to a defined topic or specific author. As with PsycINFO, you may not always find links to copies of the articles on Google Scholar, but you may find articles that were not found in a search of PsycINFO. Because Google Scholar will search for articles on many different topics, you are not limited to what is categorized in a particular database (e.g., you can find articles that are in both PsycINFO and PubMed in Google Scholar). With search engines, though, you are also more likely to come across articles that have not been peer reviewed (see below for more discussion of peer review). Articles that have not been peer reviewed are typically less reliable sources of information, because they have not been evaluated by experts in the field who verify the quality of the study.

Other search engines may yield information on a topic, but the veracity of that information may vary. Whereas PsycINFO and Google Scholar yield peer-reviewed articles on a topic, most search engines produce other types of information, such as popular press articles that may or may not report research findings accurately. Thus, a search of a database such as PsycINFO or Google Scholar is a necessary step in any literature review. Simply typing your topic into Google or Wikipedia will not provide an adequate search for a literature review. The sources that are represented in such searches are not reliable enough to use to design a study or to write a research report of a study (more on writing research reports is presented in Chapter 8).

Wikipedia provides unverified information on a topic that is too general for use in a literature review and a normal Google search of the web will not provide a thorough search of the articles on your topic, as many are not freely available on the web. You will also likely find sources that are not reliable with a Google search. In other words, Google web searches and Wikipedia searches are how *not* to do a literature review.

Finally, psychology conferences can provide a way to get the most up-to-date information about research conducted in an area (often so new that it has not been published yet). If you are unable to attend such a conference yourself, you can often search the program of these conferences online to view titles, authors, and abstracts or research studies that will be or have been presented at the conference. Some of the larger conferences that cover many areas of psychology are the American Psychological Association (APA) Convention (typically held in August each year) and the Association for Psychological Science Convention (typically held in May each year). In addition, there are many area-wide psychological association conferences for all areas of psychology (the Midwestern Psychological Association, the Southeastern Psychological Association, the Western Psychological Association, etc.) that can be found on the APA web page (www.apa.org) under News & Events. Many areas of psychology also hold annual conventions (a quick web search will yield some of these meetings and sites).

WHAT YOU FIND IN A LITERATURE REVIEW

As described above, a PsycINFO search (or a search with one of the other sources) provides you with a list of journal articles and/or book chapters that are relevant to your topic. How can these sources help you as you attempt to make a prediction about your research question? As you read the articles, you may find important information for your literature review in different sections of the articles. Before you complete your literature review, becoming familiar with the structure of different types of articles and what type of information you can expect to get from the different sections helps you complete your literature review more easily. Thus, we discuss here the structure of some of the different article types. We begin by describing journal articles.

What Is a Journal Article?

An empirical journal article is written by a researcher (or multiple researchers in many cases) to describe a research study to others who might be interested in knowing what the researcher did (someone like you if you are conducting a literature review on the researcher's topic). The researcher's article may describe a single study (e.g., one experiment) or it may describe multiple studies, all of which relate to the same research question. After the researcher has written the article, the researcher submits it to a psychological journal to attempt to get it published. If the article is published, it will be cataloged in PsycINFO, PsycARTICLES, or another database if the journal topic is primarily outside of psychology. The article is typically sent out to several reviewers who are experts on the general topic of the article (i.e., they are researchers who have done studies on the topic in the past). This is a process known as peer review. These reviewers make

Peer Review: a process that takes place prior to publication of an article in many journals where experts make suggestions for improving an article and make a recommendation about whether an article should be published in the journal

recommendations about revisions to the article to improve it and indicate whether or not they feel the journal should publish the article. The editor of the journal uses these reviews to decide if the article can be published in the journal and which revisions are most important. The author of the article then revises the article or may attempt to submit it to a different journal (if the editor has decided not to publish the article in that particular journal). If the revised article is submitted to the same journal, it may then be reviewed again, or it may be accepted by the editor for publication. The review process can be lengthy (sometimes taking many months or even a year), but it is important in verifying the quality of the study before it is published. Thus, articles that are not peer reviewed may describe studies of lower quality. If you conduct only a simple Google search of the web for your literature review, you may find only some of these unpublished articles. After the article is accepted for publication, it can then take a few more months before the article appears in the journal. Consequently, articles are rarely published very soon after they are written, which means that research is already a year or more old before it is published.

Empirical journal articles are considered primary sources for research information because they are written by the researchers who conducted the research and details of the study are provided. Journal articles differ from popular magazine articles. Popular magazine articles often contain short summaries of the study written by an author other than the primary source (i.e., they are secondary sources) and may not provide an accurate account of the study in all cases. Thus, popular magazine articles are considered secondary sources. An accurate and thorough literature review requires review of primary sources (i.e., journal articles).

Many areas of psychology have journals devoted to research on a particular topic, but there are also journals that publish research in all areas of psychology. Table 2.3 provides a list of some general psychology journals, as well as journals that specialize in a particular area. In most cases, you can figure out what types of studies are published in the journal from the title of the journal.

Table 2.3   A List of Psychological Journals by Type of Article Published

General psychology journals—these journals publish studies from various areas of psychology

Psychological Science

Journal of Experimental Psychology: General

Journal of Experimental Psychology: Applied

American Psychologist

Canadian Journal of Experimental Psychology

Experimental Psychology

Personality and social psychology

Journal of Personality and Social Psychology

Journal of Experimental Social Psychology

Personality and Social Psychology Bulletin

Personality and Individual Differences

Journal of Research in Personality

(Continued)

Table 2.3 (Continued)

Cognitive psychology
Journal of Experimental Psychology: Learning, Memory, and Cognition
Journal of Experimental Psychology: Human Perception and Performance
Cognition
Journal of Memory and Language
Memory and Cognition
Applied Cognitive Psychology
Developmental psychology
Journal of Experimental Child Psychology
Child Development
Psychology and Aging
Developmental Psychology
British Journal of Developmental Psychology
Biological psychology
Neuropsychology
Neuropsychologia
Applied Neuropsychology
Review and theoretical journals—these journals publish review articles and/or articles describing new or revised theories about behavior (some of these journals publish empirical studies as well)
Psychological Review
Psychological Bulletin
Psychonomic Bulletin & Review
Developmental Review
Best Practices in School Psychology
Behavioral and Brain Sciences

Structure of an Empirical Journal Article

Journal articles are organized into sections. Each section provides specific information about a study. Each major section of a journal article is described in this section.

Abstract: a summary of an article that appears at the beginning of the article and in searchable databases of journal articles

Abstract. As described earlier, an abstract is a short summary of the study that allows readers to decide if the article is relevant to their literature review without their reading the entire article. Abstracts of articles are cataloged in PsycINFO. They are typically 120 to 150 words long (strict APA style allows a maximum of 120 words—see Chapter 8 for more information about APA style) and include a sentence or two summarizing each of the major sections of the article. Thus, the abstract usually includes (a) the general topic of the study, (b) a brief description of the methodology, (c) the major results of the study, and (d) what was learned from the study.

Introduction. As the title implies, the Introduction section of the article introduces the topic, research question, and other relevant information for the study. If an introduction is written well, it should contain the following information:

- Introduction to the general topic of the study (e.g., the bystander effect)
- General problem that the study addresses (e.g., factors that affect the bystander effect)
- Discussion of relevant background studies that inform the researchers about what is known about the problem and how these studies are related to the present study the researchers are describing in their article (e.g., studies that were found in a literature review of factors that affect the bystander effect)
- Justification of the present study (i.e., what aspect of the research question the present study will answer that has not been determined from past studies)
- Brief description of how the current study addresses the relevant aspect of the research question (may include variables that are being studied and a short outline of the method of the study)
- Predictions (i.e., hypotheses) that the researchers made about the outcome of the present study

The introduction should essentially make an argument about what the present study will contribute to knowledge in the selected area of psychology and why the researchers made their hypotheses. If you can identify the points of support for the authors' argument, then you probably have a reasonable understanding of the important information in the introduction.

> **Introduction:** a section of an APA-style article that introduces the topic of the study, reviews relevant background studies, and presents predictions for the data
>
> **Method:** section of an APA-style article that describes the participants, design, stimuli, apparatus, and procedure used in the study

Method. The purpose of the Method section is to provide enough information about how a study was conducted so that others can evaluate and (if they wish) reproduce the study to see if the results replicate. There are four subsections of the Method: Participants (also called *Subjects* in non-APA-style journals or if animal subjects are used), Design, Materials, and Procedure. The Participants subsection describes who the participants in the study were (How many were there? Were they college students? How many males and females participated? If they were animal subjects, what species were they?). How the participants for the study are obtained is also described (Did they volunteer from a participant pool? Were they recruited on a website? If they were animal subjects, were they bred by the researcher?). The Design subsection describes the design of the study (What were the variables studied? How were they studied?). The Materials subsection describes the various materials and apparatus that were used in the study (If there were stimuli shown to the participants, what were the stimuli? If a survey was used, what kinds of items did it include?).

The Procedure subsection provides a chronological description of what the participants did in the study (What were their tasks? What instructions were they given? How many trials did the participants complete?). Sometimes authors will combine some of these subsections (e.g., Design and Materials) as the information in these sections can overlap. In very short empirical articles (e.g., *Psychological Science* short reports), the subsections will all be combined into one large Method section.

❦

Results: section of an APA-style article that presents a summary of the results and the statistical tests of the predictions

Discussion: section of an APA-style article that compares the results of a study to the predictions and the results of previous studies

---

Results. The Results section provides a summary of the data (often in tables or figures) and information about the statistical tests that were performed to analyze the data. The findings are described in the text with statistical values given as support for the findings described. The specific types of values given depend on the type of tests the researchers conducted. Thus, if the tests themselves are not familiar to you, focus on the description the authors provide of the findings. Were there group differences? Was there a relationship between the behaviors measured? Look back at what the authors expected to find to see if you can match their findings to their predictions.

Discussion. The last section of the article is the Discussion section. The authors go back to their predictions and discuss their findings in reference to their predictions. If the findings support their predictions, the authors indicate what they learned about the research question and perhaps where researchers should go next in this area. If the findings do not support their predictions, they should describe some possible explanations for why they did not support the predictions. A discussion of the results in the context of previous findings is also included. Finally, a summary of what was learned from the study should be included in the Discussion section, including possible limitations of these conclusions based on strengths and weaknesses of the study conducted. Researchers may also suggest a direction for future research in that area.

Multiple Experiment/Study Articles. Many articles that are published include more than one study that addresses the same research question. In this case, the article includes one Introduction that provides the background and motivation for all the studies. It may also include short introductions to each study/experiment to describe the motivation for each study separately. The article also includes separate Method and Results sections for each study. The Results section for each study also includes a short Discussion section for that study, but a General Discussion section concludes the article that then ties all the studies together.

Review Articles and Book Chapters

Most of the articles you come across in a literature review are empirical journal articles as described above. However, a smaller set of articles may be found that fit into the categories of review article or book chapter. The purpose of these articles is to organize and summarize research in a particular area of psychology to give researchers a review of the research to date. Accordingly, these sorts of articles can be very useful in a literature review because they allow a researcher to find a lot of information about a topic in a single article. These reviews also provide a list of references that can be helpful in searching for empirical articles about specific studies that may be important for developing a prediction for the researcher's study. The main difference between review articles and book chapters is where they are published. Some psychological journals are devoted entirely to review articles (see Table 2.3 for some examples). There are also journals that reserve a small portion of space for review articles (e.g., *Psychonomic Bulletin & Review*). Review articles go through the same rigorous review process as that for empirical journal articles (described above). Book chapters are typically published in a book that is either entirely written by a set of authors (i.e., every chapter is written by the authors) or in an edited book where editors compile chapters on a similar topic from multiple authors. The review process for book chapters is variable and may not be as rigorous as that for journal articles.

Stop and Think

(2.3) What is the purpose of a journal article?

(2.4) How can reading journal articles aid in a literature review?

(2.5) In what way(s) can peer review affect the quality of a journal article?

(2.6) Briefly describe the major sections of a journal article.

USING THE LITERATURE TO MAKE HYPOTHESES

The primary goals of a literature review are to (a) determine what research has been done on a research question to avoid duplicating previous research and (b) review previous findings and theories to allow a hypothesis to be made about the outcome of a study. A hypothesis is the prediction for the findings of the study. For example, a researcher might hypothesize that a relationship exists between two measures of behavior. For a different type of study, a researcher might predict that one group of participants will have average scores that are higher than the average scores of another group. There are two primary types of information that researchers use to make hypotheses from a literature review: theories and previous results. These types of information result in theory-driven hypotheses and data-driven hypotheses. However, regardless of the types of hypotheses that are developed, hypotheses should be stated as specifically as possible in terms of how behaviors and conditions are related (Figure 2.4).

Hypothesis: prediction regarding the results of a research study

Theory-Driven Hypothesis: hypothesis for a study that is based on a theory about the behavior of interest

Data-Driven Hypothesis: hypothesis for a study that is based on the results of previous, related studies

Figure 2.4   Steps in the Research Process: Developing a Hypothesis

Figure 2.4   Steps in the Research Process: Developing a Hypothesis

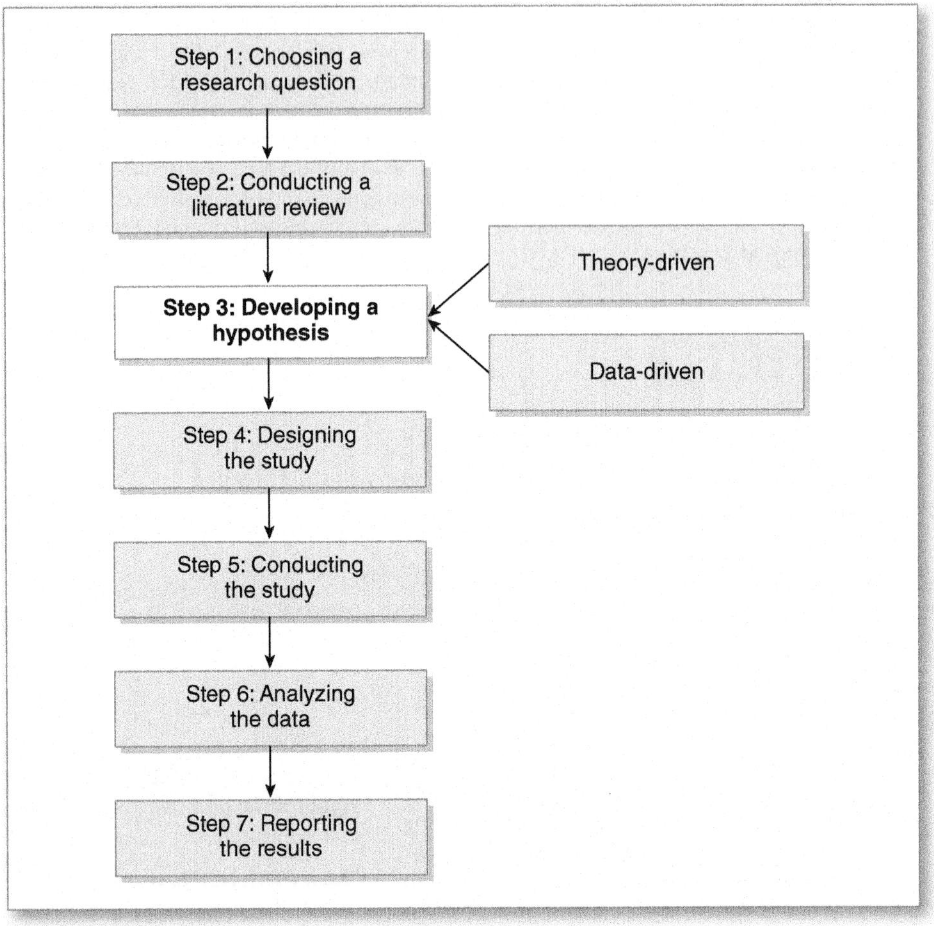

Theory-Driven Hypotheses

Theory-driven hypotheses are made from the predictions of a theory. These are typically made for studies designed to test a theory (i.e., look for data that support or falsify a theory—see the Testability section in Chapter 1). For example, suppose a theory has been proposed that anxiety causes insomnia. A researcher conducting a study to test this theory might then predict that if two groups of participants are compared, one that is put in an anxiety-provoking situation and one that is put in a relaxing situation, the anxious group will report more problems sleeping than the relaxed group. In other words, the researcher might predict that the anxious group, on average, will report fewer hours of sleep per night than the relaxed group. This hypothesis would be consistent with the theory that anxiety causes insomnia and is therefore a theory-driven hypothesis. A theory-driven hypothesis involves deductive reasoning in that a researcher is taking a general statement about behavior (the theory) and making a specific prediction (the hypothesis) about the study from this general statement.

Deductive Reasoning: using general information to make a specific prediction

Another example of a theory-driven hypothesis can be seen in a recent study on face perception. Sofer, Dotsch, Wigboldus, and Todorov (2015, Experiment 1) tested a theory that the typicality of a face is important in social evaluations of a person. From this theory, the researchers hypothesized that more typical faces would be judged as more trustworthy, because trustworthiness is an important part of social interaction. To test the hypothesis, they conducted a study where female students were presented with female faces created from composites of two faces: an attractive female face and a typical female face (see Figure 2.5). Thus, the faces ranged from highly typical to highly attractive depending on the amount of each of the two original faces present in the composite. Subjects in the study were asked to judge both the attractiveness and the trustworthiness of each face. The results were consistent with their hypothesis: The more typical the face was, the higher the ratings of trustworthiness from the participants. The attractiveness ratings supported their prediction as well, as the less typical faces were judged as more attractive and less trustworthy than the more typical faces. Thus, their study supported the hypothesis that typical faces are judged as more trustworthy, which provided support for the theory that the typicality of a face is important in social evaluations.

Figure 2.5 Faces Used to Create Stimuli in the Sofer et al. (2015) Study. Photo (a) Shows a Typical Face and Photo (b) Shows an Attractive Face

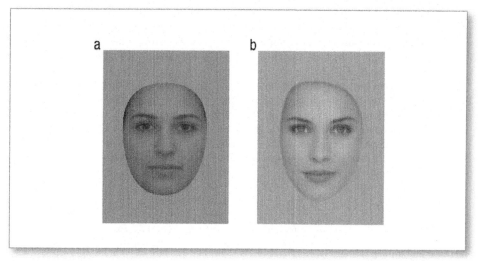

SOURCE: Figure 1 from Sofer et al. (2015).

Now, consider how the process of a literature review can aid you in developing research questions and hypotheses for your studies. Suppose you are interested in the origin of math abilities and you are conducting a literature review on the development of mathematical concepts and you found that a researcher had suggested the theory that understanding of mathematical operations (e.g., addition, subtraction) is innate (something children are born with). Can you think of a way to make a theory-driven hypothesis for a study that tests this theory? Think about how the study would be conducted and then use the theory to make a hypothesis about the outcome of the study (an example of how this could be done is presented after the Test Yourself section at the end of this chapter).

Data-Driven Hypotheses

Another way in which researchers can make hypotheses about a study is by examining the specific findings of previous studies that are similar and generalizing the findings to their study. Hypotheses made in this way are considered data-driven hypotheses because they are made based on data from previous studies. This type of hypothesis involves inductive reasoning because the researcher is taking a specific result from another study and using it to make a more general prediction for the research question of interest. For example, suppose researchers are interested in causes of insomnia. In their literature review, they come across a study that found that people who report high levels of anxiety also report getting less sleep per night. From this study's results, they may conclude that anxiety is related to insomnia and make the hypothesis for their study that a relationship between level of anxiety and number of hours of sleep will be found.

Inductive Reasoning: using specific information to make a more general prediction

A study by Schnall, Benton, and Harvey (2008) provides an example of a hypothesis based on data from previous studies. These researchers were interested in the connection between emotions and moral judgments. Previous studies had shown that when participants were induced to feel disgust (e.g., exposed to a bad smell), they judged an action as more immoral than control participants who did not experience the disgusting situation (Schnall, Haidt, Clore, & Jordan, 2008). Schnall, Benton, and Harvey (2008) hypothesized from these results that, if feelings of cleanliness were induced, the opposite effect should occur: Participants should judge actions less harshly. They conducted two experiments to test this data-driven hypothesis. In both experiments, one group of participants was primed with the concept of cleanliness, while another group was not primed with this concept. Participants then judged the actions of others in a set of moral dilemmas (e.g., keeping money in a found wallet). Results indicated that participants who experienced the concept of cleanliness in the study rated the actions in the dilemmas less harshly than participants who were not primed with the concept. Thus, Schnall et al. supported their data-driven hypothesis with the results of their study.

Descriptive and Causal Hypotheses

Regardless of where the information comes from, hypotheses will either attempt to describe behavior or make a causal prediction about behavior. This distinction maps on to the different types of research questions described above: descriptive and causal. Which type of research question is being asked will also dictate which type of hypothesis is made: a descriptive hypothesis or a causal hypothesis. If researchers are interested in the causes of behavior, they state a prediction about a particular cause of behavior, typically as a difference in groups or conditions that differ based on the cause being studied. For example, if researchers have the research question "Does drinking caffeine on the day of an exam cause an improvement in test performance in college students?" then their hypothesis may be that a group of students who are asked to drink caffeine the day of an

Descriptive Hypothesis: a prediction about the results of a study that describes the behavior or the relationship between behaviors

Causal Hypothesis: a prediction about the results of a study that includes the causes of a behavior

exam will have higher test performance than a group of students who are asked not to drink caffeine. If, however, the researchers are interested only in whether certain behaviors occur together or wish to document the occurrence of a particular behavior, they are likely to have a descriptive research question and a descriptive hypothesis. For example, if researchers have the research question "Do students who score low on an exam also have high levels of anxiety?" then their hypothesis may be descriptive, such that a relationship between these behaviors is predicted (i.e., when these behaviors are measured together, students with lower test performance will have higher anxiety scores). As you will see in Chapter 4, descriptive and causal hypotheses are also tested with different types of research designs.

One important thing to note about testing hypotheses and theories: We can never *prove* a hypothesis or theory is correct in our research studies. The best we can do is to support or not support the hypothesis/theory from the data we observe in our study. This is due to the limitations of the research process (e.g., we are testing a small sample, our statistical tests are based on the probabilities of outcomes, etc.). We will discuss these limitations throughout the text, but know that they are part of any scientific process. The goal is not to prove facts, but to support predictions and explanations of the phenomena through the observations we make in our studies.

Stop and Think

(2.7) Explain the difference between a theory-driven and a data-driven hypothesis.

(2.8) How does a literature review help researchers make hypotheses about their study?

(2.9) Describe the difference between a theory and a hypothesis.

CHAPTER SUMMARY

Reconsider the questions from the beginning of the chapter:

- How do researchers develop a research question? Research questions come from many sources, including researchers' curiosity. However, research questions should be relevant to current knowledge in the field of study and answerable using scientific methods. A literature review helps researchers know if their research question fulfills these criteria.

- How do researchers conduct a literature review? A literature review is a thorough review of research done in an area of study. Searchable databases, such as PsycINFO and PsycARTICLES, are useful for conducting a literature review. Conducting a Google web search or using Wikipedia is *not* a good way to conduct a literature review.
- What are some useful resources for a literature review? Searchable databases that provide researchers access to empirical and review journal articles include PsycINFO, PsycARTICLES, PubMed, and ERIC. Google Scholar may also be useful in locating some of these sources.
- What will you find in a literature review? A thorough literature review produces journal articles that researchers can use to understand what types of research questions add to knowledge in a field of study, what methods researchers are currently using to answer those research questions, and the theories or past results in an area that help researchers develop hypotheses for their studies.
- What are the different types of research articles and how are they organized? Research articles are either empirical, review, or theoretical. Empirical articles describe a study conducted by the authors of the article. Review articles summarize results and methods from a particular area of study. Theoretical articles discuss new or revised theories of behavior in an area of study.
- How do we use a literature review to make hypotheses? Researchers can use theories described in journal articles to develop hypotheses, or researchers can use past studies' results to develop a hypothesis about the outcome of their study.
- What are the different types of hypotheses that a researcher can make? A researcher can make theory-driven and data-driven hypotheses.

THINKING ABOUT RESEARCH

A summary of a research study in psychology is given below. As you read the summary, think about the following questions:

1. What type of hypothesis (theory-driven or data-driven) did the authors make?

2. Do you think this is a causal or a descriptive hypothesis? How do you know?

3. Can you state the authors' research question? From the description of the study, where did this research question seem to come from?

4. If you were to conduct a literature review for their research question on PsycINFO, how would you proceed? Describe the steps you would take.

5. Write an abstract for the study in your own words that adheres to APA guidelines.

6. If you were to read an APA-style article describing this study (which you can do by finding the reference below), in which section would you find information about the paragraphs the participants read during the study? In which section would the authors report what statistical test they conducted? In which section would they indicate if their hypothesis was supported?

Research Study. Vohs, K. D., & Schooler, J. W. (2008). The value of believing in free will: Encouraging a belief in determinism increases cheating. *Psychological Science, 19,* 49–54.

Purpose of the Study. Vohs and Schooler (2008) were interested in the effects of a belief in determinism (i.e., believing that events in a person's life are not under their control) on moral behaviors. Their interest stemmed from recent findings from neuroscientists that our behaviors may be caused by factors out of our control (e.g., our genes, the functioning of our brain, our environments, etc.). They reported that a previous study (Mueller & Dweck, 1998) had found that children exert less effort in a task if they are told that their failure, in a difficult task they had previously completed, was due to their intelligence level rather than their level of effort. From this finding, Vohs and Schooler reasoned that a belief in determinism may negatively affect behavior. Thus, in their study they predicted that exposure to a deterministic argument would result in more cheating behaviors than if this belief was not promoted.

Method of the Study. Thirty college students participated in the study. Participants were randomly assigned to read one of two paragraphs taken from the same book. One of the paragraphs suggested that scientists believe that free will is an illusion. The other paragraph discussed consciousness and did not mention the topic of free will. All participants were then asked to complete a set of math problems, presented one at a time on a computer screen. Participants were asked to complete each problem. They were also told that the computer program had an error such that the answers to some of the problems may appear with the problem and that they should try to solve the problems on their own (they could make the answer disappear by pressing the space bar when the problem appeared). The researchers measured the number of times the participants pressed the space bar as a measure of cheating behavior (more presses means less cheating).

Results of the Study. The results indicated that the group that read the determinism paragraph pressed the space bar less often (about 5 times during the study) than the control group (about 10 times during the study) that read the consciousness paragraph. Figure 2.6 displays the mean space bar presses for each group.

Conclusions of the Study. From their results, Vohs and Schooler (2008) concluded that a belief in determinism (i.e., free will is an illusion) causes more immoral behavior (e.g., cheating) to be exhibited by individuals.

Figure 2.6   Mean Number of Space Bar Presses for Each Group

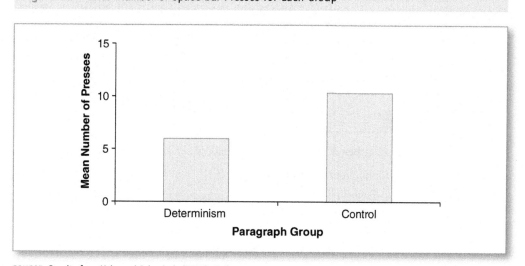

SOURCE: Results from Vohs and Schooler's (2008) study.

COMMON PITFALLS AND HOW TO AVOID THEM

Problem: Using inappropriate search engines—students often use common search engines such as Google, Yahoo, and Wikipedia to search for information about psychological research, which is unreliable and incomplete.

Solution: Use databases such as PsycINFO, PsycARTICLES, ERIC, and PubMed to search for primary source journal articles about psychological research.

Problem: Use of inappropriate sources—sometimes students include sources in literature reviews that are either not peer reviewed or are not the most relevant sources for the research question of interest.

Solution: Check the type of publication for sources (this information is provided by PsycINFO) to ensure that sources included in a literature review are the most appropriate for the research question.

Problem: Hypotheses stated too generally—students often state hypotheses for studies too generally without addressing specific aspects of the study.

Solution: Attempt to state hypotheses as specifically as possible, including variables of the study when appropriate (see Chapter 4 for more information on variables).

Problem: Focus on full-text articles—oftentimes students will focus a literature review too heavily on articles with full text access online, missing important studies for their topic.

Solution: Be sure to conduct a thorough literature review, even if that means walking over to the library to pick up a hard copy of an article that does not have full text available online.

Problem: Reading only the abstract—because the abstract contains a summary of the article, students sometimes believe that they can fully understand the article by reading just the abstract.

Solution: Abstracts are written to provide a short summary of the article and may not fully represent the method or results of a study. Thus, it is important to read through the entire article when conducting a literature review. In addition, you should never cite a source that you have not fully read.

TEST YOURSELF

1. For the information listed below, indicate in which section(s) of a journal article it should be found.

   (a) Average scores for different groups in a study
   (b) Number of participants in the study
   (c) Researchers' hypotheses
   (d) Comparison of results of present study with results of previous studies
   (e) Summary of the instructions given to the participants

2. Describe how theory-driven and data-driven hypotheses are made.

3. Explain why the research question below is not an appropriate research question for psychological research:

   Does every human being have a soul?

4. What is a *peer-reviewed journal article*, and how does it differ from an article you might find in a popular magazine?

5. What is a literature review, and why is it an important part of the research process?

6. Explain the differences between a database such as PsycINFO and a search engine such as Google.

7. A short summary of a journal article that appears at the beginning of the article and in databases such as PsycINFO is called a(n) _____.

8. Creating a theory-driven hypothesis involves _____ reasoning.

9. A hypothesis that proposes a link between exercise and memory would be classified as a _____ hypothesis.

10. What is the difference between an empirical journal article and a book chapter or review article?

Answers can be found at edge.sagepub/mcbride3e.

Example of Theory-Driven Hypothesis for Innateness of Mathematical Operations (From the section "Theory-Driven Hypotheses"): To determine that something is innate, you would need to test infants who are very young and have not had enough experience with objects to develop an understanding of mathematical operations such as addition and subtraction. You could then test these infants in a study where you show them objects of a set number that they are habituated to (no longer show interest in), occlude the objects with a screen, and then either add an object or remove an object behind the screen so that the infant can see the object being added or subtracted. You then remove the screen and show them the objects, but show them an incorrect number of objects based on the operation. If the infants show interest (indicating something that was not expected by the infants) in what they are shown, this can be seen as evidence that the infants understand what they should have seen after the operation was performed. Thus, the theory-driven hypothesis for this study is that infants will look longer when the number of objects does not match the operation than when the number of objects does match the operation.

A study like this was performed by Wynn (1992), where her findings indicated that infants as young as 5 months looked longer when the number of objects did not match the operation than when the number of objects shown was correct based on the operation. Wynn argued that these results support the theory that understanding of addition and subtraction operations is innate.

STOP AND THINK ANSWERS

(2.1) (a) descriptive

(b) causal

(c) causal

(2.2) A literature review helps researchers determine what the open questions still are in a field, what hypotheses they should make and what methodologies work best in that area.

(2.3) The purpose of a journal article is to report to others what was found in a research study.

(2.4) Reading journal articles can help researchers determine what research questions they should ask, what hypotheses they should make, and what methodologies work best in that area.

(2.5) Peer review is conducted to improve the quality of a journal article by having experts in an area provide suggestions to improve the writing, research, or conclusions of the authors. It also helps determine whether a study gets published or not.

(2.6) Abstract—short summary; Introduction—provides research questions, hypotheses, and relevant background and purpose for a study; Method—provides details of the methodology such that other researchers could replicate the study if they wish; Results—summarizes data collected in a study and provides tests of the hypotheses from the data; Discussion—describes conclusions from the results of the study; References—provides full references for all sources cited in a paper

(2.7) Theory-driven hypotheses are ones based on a theory or description of how behavior works. Data-driven hypotheses are based on results from similar, past studies. Some hypotheses are based on both theory and past results.

(2.8) Reading journal articles can help a researcher make both theory-driven and data-driven hypotheses.

(2.9) A theory is a description of how behavior operates. A hypothesis is a prediction about how results will turn out in a study that might provide a test of a theory.

⑤SAGE edge™

Visit edge.sagepub.com/mcbride3e for the tools you need to sharpen your study skills:

- Web Quizzes
- eFlashcards
- Thinking About Research

- SAGE Journal Articles
- Web and Multimedia Resources

Ethical Considerations and the BPS Code of Conduct

6

Harrison, E. and Rentzelas, P.

As psychologists, we need to make sure that we adhere to the British Psychological Society Code of Ethics and Conduct at all times in research and in practice.

The British Psychological Society recognises its obligation to set and uphold the highest standards of professionalism, and to promote ethical behaviour, attitudes and judgements on the part of psychologists by:

- being mindful of the need for protection of the public;
- expressing clear ethical principles, values and standards;
- promoting such standards by education and consultation;
- developing and implementing methods to help psychologists monitor their professional behaviour and attitudes;
- assisting psychologists with ethical decision making;
- providing opportunities for discourse on these issues.

The Code of Ethics and Conduct has been regularly updated since it was adopted in 1985, and should guide all members of the British Psychological Society. It should be read in conjunction with the Society's Royal Charter, Statutes and Rules. The latest version of the Code of Ethics and Conduct (2009) at the time of printing this book, can be found at: http://beta.bps.org.uk/sites/beta.bps.org.uk/files/Policy%20-%20Files/Code%20of%20Ethics%20and%20Conduct%20%282009%29.pdf

The ethical review process
Why do we need to apply for ethical approval?
We have a duty of care to uphold the University's reputation regarding ethical guidelines. Every time you conduct a research project, whether as an undergraduate, postgraduate, researcher, or academic, you will need to submit an ethical approval application to the ethics committee.

The ethical application process is an important part of the dissertation, because you cannot collect data without prior ethical approval. You need this in order to complete your dissertation, and you need to pass your dissertation in order to gain BPS accreditation from your degree.

If we conduct research incorrectly and don't adhere to ethical issues there may also be legal implications, which we need to avoid. You will need to consider all of these implications when making your application, and address any issues that may arise before beginning the data collection process.

Principles and laws

There are certain principles that we need to adhere to when applying for ethical approval and conducting the research. These principles are often defined by the relevant regulatory body – in Psychology these principles are outlined by the BPS.

The BPS Code of Human Research Ethics sets out the general principles that are applicable to all research contexts and are intended to cover all research with human participants. The Code explains that researchers should respect the rights and dignity of participants in their research and the legitimate interests of stakeholders, by adhering to certain principles. The latest version of the Code of Human Research Ethics at the time of publishing this book can be found at: http://www.bps.org.uk/sites/default/files/documents/code_of_human_research_ethics.pdf

As well as the Code of Human Research Ethics, it is important to recognise that internet-mediated research is becoming more and more popular. If you wish to conduct your research online, the BPS has produced some newer guidelines for internet mediated research and conducting research in internet based domains: http://www.bps.org.uk/system/files/Public%20files/inf206-guidelines-for-internet-mediated-research.pdf

The Economic and social research council (ESRC) (http://www.esrc.ac.uk/) and the Research Councils UK (RCUK) (http://www.rcuk.ac.uk/) also provide some ethical guidelines that are not specific to Psychology. These guidelines may help to gauge ethical principles more generally, and may be useful when referring to more general applications of some of the principles outlined by the BPS.

In addition to Codes of Conduct, there is also certain documentation and legislation which we must adhere to as professionals. The Data Protection Act is one example. We must adhere to the rules of the Data Protection Act when discussing the storage and protection of your data, particularly in relation to the personal information of your participants and the data you have obtained from them. We will cover data storage later when we discuss the ethical approval application process. Secondly, we must adhere to the principles of the Safeguarding Vulnerable Groups Act, which is all about protecting participants who may be part of a vulnerable group. If you are conducting research that involves contact with vulnerable groups, you will need to go through the Disclosure and Barring Service (DBS) to make sure that you are fit to conduct research with them. This applies for anyone who is under the age of 18, or those over 18 with difficulties or disabilities which mean they may not be able to provide full consent, for example if you want to conduct research within a school or with patients with mental health conditions.

Minimising risk

One of the most important parts of the ethical review process is addressing the concept of risk. We need to identify and minimise any physical and psychological risks to both the participants and to you as the researcher. It is important to recognise that there is never no risk at all – There is always some risk, not matter how small. So, on the section of the form that asks you about risks, you should state that the risk is minimal, and justify why. Alternatively, if you identify any substantial risks (physical or psychological) you should explain what precautions you will take to minimise these risks.

It is important to address potential risks in line with the relevant standards of practice outlined by the BPS, such as Duty of Care and Respect of the participants' confidentiality and privacy.

The application form

The BCU psychology department ethical approval application form addresses the following areas:

1. project details
2. study background
3. vulnerable groups
4. permission to collect data
5. general ethical consideration
6. sensitive topics
7. benefits and risks
8. data protection

We will now discuss each of these areas in more detail.

1. Project details

The first section is an administration section which the ethics board will complete for their records, so you can leave this blank. You will need to complete the information about project dates, project title, and your contact details, and provide details on all locations where data will be collected. This applies for both face to face and online data collection.

2. Study background

Within the study background section you will need to provide reference to existing literature and outline the background of your study and the rationale for your project. In the design section, explain the type of study you are conducting and the research strategy you will employ, for example, is it a questionnaire design? Experimental design? Longitudinal? How are your groups defined? Are you conducting within/between groups design? Or if qualitative, what are you looking at and how will you assess it? e.g. with interviews?

The primary outcome is the main variable you are aiming to measure, i.e. your dependent variable(s). For example, if you are looking at the impact of exams on student stress levels, your main outcome would be stress. In qualitative research you may not be assessing a particular variable, but you may be exploring a particular topic, for example participant's transition to university. You also need to outline you research question(s), addressing whether you are looking at the differences between or within groups, e.g. the difference between males and females on a particular measure. For qualitative designs, you may be conducting an exploration of people's experiences of a particular life event.

Any measures you use, whether these are questionnaires, interview schedules, scales or tests, all need to be mentioned on the ethics application. If you are using previously established measures then you need to explain these, including details on reliability and some examples of the questions. If you have developed your own scales, then these also need to be explained in full, with details on how they were developed. For example if you have devised your own interview schedule or questionnaire, why have you focused on specific topic areas? Were these areas based on previous literature? You should also give some idea of content by providing examples of the questions. It is important to also make sure you attach copies of the measures to your ethics application so that your reviewer(s) can approve these.

Finally in this section, the sample size needs to be explained and justified. You may want to refer to previous research that has used a similar sample size, or you may have conducted a power analysis using G-power to determine a suitable sample size for your research. If you do not justify your sample size and later discover that you have not collected enough data, the data set would not be valid and it would be a waste of the participants' time. It is therefore important to make sure that you consider this in the planning stage.

3. Vulnerable groups

Within this section you should consider how you will be interacting with the participants in your study. For example, if you are working with vulnerable adults or children under the age of 18. You should consider how you will minimise any risks that may arise from working with such groups, and how you will protect both your participant(s) and yourself as the researcher. The concept of risk will be addressed later in the form. If you declare here that you will be working with any vulnerable groups then you will need to apply for a DBS check in advance, and provide your certificate number on the ethical application form within the section on 'Permission to collect data'. If you are planning to go into an external organisation to collect your data, for example in a school, you also need to provide an indication that you are allowed to collect data there by providing evidence of gatekeeper permission. This will normally be provided in the form of a letter explaining that the organisation has approved your study and that they are happy for you to collect your data with them.

4. General ethical considerations

Inclusion and exclusion criteria need to be outlined on your ethical approval application. It is important to recognise that certain individuals may be particularly vulnerable in certain studies. For example, someone who has had an eating disorder may be excluded from a study on eating behaviour. These individuals may be excluded because ethical implications may be too complex, particularly for an undergraduate study. Similarly, groups that could systematically bias the findings of the study may also be excluded, for example, people who have a specific disability may be excluded as they may perform differently to a normally developing population on particular tasks. It is important that you consider all potential issues with recruitment of certain individuals, and the impact that recruitment could have on your study in general and on your data.

You also need to address how participants will be recruited. Consider how you will advertise your study, how you will recruit participants, and what your sampling technique will be. Make sure you provide enough detail for risk assessment.

It is also important to consider how you will gain informed consent from your participants. Explain here that you will provide participant information sheets, consent forms, and give your participants the opportunity to ask questions (and remember to attach all of the forms to the application!) Consider how the informed consent process will work if participants are being gathered from a vulnerable population, for example if you are working with participants under the age of 18 you will need to gain permission from their parents/guardians. Also consider how this process will work if you are conducting your study in an online environment. This process will be different to a face-to-face study, as it can be difficult to ensure that participants have read all the relevant information before consenting to take part.

Also consider what actions you will take if a participant becomes distressed or uncomfortable within the research environment. How will you identify that participants may have lost the ability to consent to taking part, and how will you respond to this?

5. Sensitivity

If you are conducting research on a sensitive topic, you will need to provide some detail about risks of sensitive information. Issues such as death, crime, personal health and safety, amongst other issues, may arise during the course of your project. Remember that there is never a situation where there is absolutely no risk at all. Even if you are working in a seemingly safe environment and discussing seemingly neutral topics, something could trigger a participant to respond in an unexpected way and reveal unexpected information. Your ethical approval application therefore needs to explain what you would do if anything of this nature arose during your study and who you would contact.

6. Benefits and risks

You need to identify what outcomes could occur for your participants, including any benefits and risks. Benefits are any physical or psychological reward, for example, some studies may provide an incentive for taking part, such as vouchers or snacks. If this is something that applies to your study, you need to explain this here. Even if you are not providing any incentive, participants may gain a psychological reward through learning about the topic area and contributing to research and knowledge in the area.

Risks also need to be identified, however small they may be, and these risks need to be assessed based on the impact they could have on your participants, both physically and psychologically. For example, there is always a risk that participants may feel uncomfortable with some of the topics discussed or assessed in your study, and you will need to explain what you will do to minimise these risks.

Follow the same process for personal risk to yourself. There is always some potential risk depending on how the participant may respond to your study, and you need to explain how you will protect yourself from physical and psychological harm as a researcher. It is important to consider this in the ethics application because the university has a duty of care to you as a researcher, and therefore the ethics committee can't let you do anything that could put you in danger. For this reason, if you later make any changes to your study after gaining ethical approval, for example if you decide to conduct your research in a different environment, you will need to submit an ethics amendment to the committee so that they can approve that these changes are still ethical.

7. Data protection

Finally, you need to consider how you will protect the details of your participants in line with the Data Protection Act. This is both an ethical and legal implication. You need to ensure that participants are anonymous, and/or that the data is confidential at the very least. A lot of people get confused between these two terms and use the terms interchangeably, so let us explain the difference:

- Anonymous: This is when even you as a researcher won't be able to identify an individual participant and that participant's responses. There *are* ways to make the data completely anonymous, but the problem is that if the participant is completely anonymous, they will not be able to withdraw their data as you will not be able to identify them or their data. There are ethical implications with this, so most people will go with confidentiality rather than complete anonymity.
- Confidentiality: The best way to ensure confidentiality is to provide participants with a participant code or number, so that their names will not be recorded anywhere other than

on the consent form. This way, if you need to locate the data of an individual participant you can go back to the data set and find it using the code or number on their consent form. Remember that if you are using this method, the consent forms and raw data need to be stored separately and securely.

Online studies will have their own ethical implications surrounding risks against anonymity and confidentiality and it is important that you consider the specifics of this in the context of your individual study.

If you are conducting qualitative research, you can ensure confidentiality by providing a pseudonym for participants during interviews. It is important *never* to record the participant's real names at any point during transcription, and also to retract or provide pseudonyms for the names of others that may be mentioned during the interview(s).

General rules surrounding data protection depend on the type of study you are conducting. You should consider the types of data you are collecting and how you can withdraw data if a participant wishes to withdraw. Also consider who has access to the data, as it might not just be you as the main researcher, your supervisor will likely have access too. If you are using external organisations such as schools, they may request a copy of your data set as well.

The application process

You should work with your supervisor to make sure that your application is clear and that you have fully explained all considerations. You will need to complete the form as part of your formative proposal, so you need to start thinking about this early. Once your supervisor is satisfied that you have addressed all areas of the form sufficiently, it should then be signed off ready to submit to the ethics committee.

The application will be reviewed by the Ethic's Chair and other staff members. There are 4 possible outcomes from your application:

1. Approval
2. Minor ethical amendments (Chair's approval)
3. Minor typographical or procedural amendments (Supervisor's approval)
4. Resubmit (for major ethical issues)

You will usually be expected to make amendments within **14 days** of receiving a response from the ethics committee. Remember you **cannot** begin collecting data until you have **full ethical approval**.

Writing Clearly

Kail, R. V.

If you asked me to describe what I did for lunch today, I might write the following:

(1a) After returning from the gym, I had my usual lunch: a sandwich, an apple, and a Diet Coke.

Alternatively, I might describe lunch like this:

(1b) After a return from the site of physical activity, consumption of a sandwich, an apple, and a Diet Coke was accomplished by me.

Had I actually written sentence 1b you probably would have thought me pompous, pretentious, or just plain strange. Yet when they move from writing about lunch to writing about research, too often writers assume they should abandon the straightforward style of sentence 1a in favor of the stilted text of sentence 1b.

Consider this pair of sentences:

(2a) The demonstration of contextual influence on visual perception is the primary contribution of this report.

(2b) Our primary finding is that context influences how people perceive visual stimuli.

Sentence 2a is the sort of sentence that's common in reports published in psychological journals, but sentence 2b expresses the same idea in language that's more direct and easier to understand.

Similarly, compare sentences 3a and 3b.

(3a) Overestimation of negative reactions to unpleasant outcomes is common because of underestimation of adjustment to those outcomes.

(3b) People often overestimate how negatively they will respond to unpleasant outcomes because they underestimate their ability to adjust to those outcomes.

The idea that's obscure in sentence 3a is crystal clear in sentence 3b.

In this lesson we'll see how to write sentences like 1a, 2b, and 3b, which are clear, concrete, and direct, and how to avoid sentences like 1b, 2a, and 3a, which are vague, abstract, and obscure. We'll start by looking at a primary symptom of obscure writing and then consider strategies for writing clearly.

What Makes Some Writing Hard to Read?

Sentences 1b, 2a, and 3a represent a kind of writing that's often known as *bureaucratese* or *academese*, depending on the author's profession. The hallmark of such writing is the frequent presence of nominalizations, nouns derived from verbs or adjectives. Nominalizations often end in *-tion, -ment, -ence,* and *-ness.* For example, *organization, recruitment, prominence,* and *brightness* are nominalizations derived from verbs (*organize, recruit*) and adjectives (*prominent, bright*). Other nominalizations found frequently in psychological writing are shown in Table 1.1.

Table 1.1   Common Nominalizations

Verb	Nominalization	Adjective	Nominalization
expect	expectation	precise	precision
perform	performance	clear	clarity
evaluate	evaluation	significant	significance
integrate	integration	different	difference

Nominalizations make writing seem obscure because they take the concrete action of a verb or the descriptive power of an adjective and bury it in a noun. Nominalizations are particularly harmful when they appear as the subject of a sentence, coupled with a weak verb, such as *is, are, seems,* or *has.* Sentence 3a illustrates this pattern: "Overestimation . . . is . . ."

Exercise 1.1

Identify the nominalizations in sentences 1b, 2a, and 3a.

A key to clear writing is recognizing nominalizations and, when possible, returning them to their original state as a verb or adjective. In fact, eliminating unnecessary nominalizations may be the single most important step in making your writing more direct and clear.

Strategies for Writing Clear, Direct Sentences

Avoiding nominalizations is good advice but not particularly satisfying because it says "what not to do" instead of "what to do." Let's return to sentences 1a and 1b (page 1). Sentence 1b is difficult because of the nominalizations, but it's not the mere absence of nominalizations that makes sentence 1a so easy to understand. Instead, sentence 1a is clear because it's a one-sentence story about a person (me) and his actions (eating lunch). As stories go, it's not much; Steven Spielberg isn't about to call for the movie rights. But it's a story nonetheless, and like much better stories by J. K. Rowling, John Grisham, and Nicholas Sparks, it's readable because it focuses on a character acting.

Storytelling may seem far removed from scientific writing, but scientific writing typically has a tale to tell. Sentence 4a is written in academese:

> (4a) The belief of in-groups is that out-group members are less intelligent and less attractive.

It has a nominalization in its subject (*belief*) that's linked to a weak verb (*is*). But there's a story lurking underneath, one about in-groups and what they believe. Consequently, if we revise the sentence so that the character is in the subject and the action is in the verb, we get something that's much clearer:

> (4b) In-groups believe that out-group members are less intelligent and less attractive.

Sentences 5a and 5b show the same pattern:

> (5a) Susceptibility to the vanishing-ball illusion seems greater in individuals with ASD.

> (5b) Individuals with ASD are more susceptible to the vanishing-ball illusion.

Sentence 5b is easier to read because it puts the character in the subject and changes the nominalization to an adjective (susceptibility→susceptible).

Exercise 1.2

Identify the characters and actions in the following sentences and then revise them with characters as subjects and actions as verbs.

1. Extraction of the gist of a scene is accomplished in a fraction of a second.
2. Counterfactual reasoning was the focus of our research.
3. Disclosure of personal information to friends is less common among East Asians than among Westerners.

The examples we've seen so far involve simple sentences that include little more than a subject, verb, and object. But the same principles follow when we move to more complex sentences that include, for example, dependent clauses like the one in sentence 6a:

(6a) Although skepticism of people who have been misleading previously is common in older children, trust in others is more frequent in pre-school children.

Sentence 6a begins with a long dependent clause about older children and then moves to the independent clause about preschool children. The clauses have the same structure: a noun phrase built around a nominalization that's linked to a weak verb: *skepticism of people . . . is* and *trust in others is.* We can make the sentence more active (and clearer) by revising to eliminate the nominalizations, replacing *skepticism* with *skeptical* and *trust* (as a noun) with *trust* (as a verb):

(6b) Although older children are skeptical of people who have misled them previously, preschool children generally trust others.

Sentence 7a is even more complex:

(7a) Given this inability to identify the long-term benefits of a positive family life, the present longitudinal investigation was conducted.

In this case, the introductory dependent clause has two nominalizations (*inability, benefits*), and the independent clause has one (*investigation*). By replacing them with verbs and adjectives, and adding characters for the verbs, the sentence becomes clearer.

(7b) Because past research has been unable to determine whether a positive family life is beneficial in the long term, we investigated this issue longitudinally.

When you run into sentences that are even longer and more complex grammatically, the same approach works: find nominalizations, replace them with verbs or adjectives, and add characters to the verbs. That said, although sentences 6b and 7b may be improvements over sentences 6a and 7a, they're far from being straightforward. In the next section we'll look at strategies for writing long sentences clearly.

Exercise 1.3

Replace the nominalizations in the following sentences with verbs or adjectives; add characters as necessary.

1. Interactions with natural elements lead to replenishment of directed-attention processes.

2. Feelings of cleanliness reduce judgments of the severity of others' moral transgressions.

3. A consonantal advantage for accuracy is well established in lexical processing.

Writing Long Sentences Clearly

Good storytelling focuses on characters and their actions: Good sentences get to characters quickly and link those characters strongly with their actions. To translate this principle into a tool for revising, remember that characters are typically introduced in the subject of a sentence; their actions are captured in the verb (and the objects of that verb). This leads directly to one rule of thumb: Effective sentences get to the subject quickly; they do not begin with long introductory clauses that force the reader to wonder what a sentence is all about. Such clauses make sentences 6b and 7b hard to understand. In 6b, for example, the story is about preschool children's beliefs, yet the reader must plow through a long clause about older children's beliefs. Similarly, in sentence 7b the story line is about the author's longitudinal study, but this surfaces only after a lengthy critique of the state of the literature.

If an introductory clause has more than five or six words, make it shorter. For example, the introductory clause in 6c has only three words, down from 12 in 6b.

(6c) Unlike older children, preschool children generally trust people who have misled them previously.

Another strategy is to eliminate the introductory clause completely, by moving it to the end of the sentence:

(7c) We investigated this issue longitudinally because past research has been unable to determine whether a positive family life is beneficial in the long term.

Exercise 1.4

Revise these sentences to eliminate the long introductory clause.

1. Because bilingual children have extensive experience selecting one language for production and inhibiting another, their cognitive control surpasses that of monolingual children.

2. Although both white and black individuals experience anxiety during interracial interactions, people can detect such anxiety only in members of their own race.

3. Given findings that prior experience helps infants segment words and that experiences associating objects and shapes help infants know that similarly shaped objects have the same name, we investigated the impact of experience on infants' mastery of syntax.

A second rule of thumb is to move directly from subject to verb to object; unnecessary words inserted between the subject and verb or between verb and object weaken the links between the key elements in the story line. Sentence 8a demonstrates this problem:

(8a) Some adults, due to attachment anxiety, are skeptical that spouses will support them in times of need.

The story is about adults who doubt that spouses will support them. The character, *adults*, is the subject of the sentence, and the action, *are skeptical*, is the verb phrase. But inserting *due to attachment anxiety* between subject and verb muddies the waters. First, it separates the character from the action. Second, it mixes the phenomenon itself (adults question their spouses' support) with its cause (some adults are anxiously attached). Fortunately, fixing this one is easy:

(8b) Due to attachment anxiety, some adults are skeptical that spouses will support them in times of need.

Due to attachment anxiety works fine as an introductory clause because it's only four words long. And removing it from the independent clause strengthens the link between the subject and verb.

Phrases inserted between verbs and objects are just as disruptive:

(9a) Experiencing power enhances, across diverse cultures, people's satisfaction with their friendships, romantic relationships, and jobs.

The story line about the impact of power on life satisfaction is inter-
rupted by a phrase, *across diverse cultures*, that deals with generality of the
phenomenon. Here, too, moving the phrase to the beginning of the sentence
solves the problem:

(9b) Across diverse cultures, experiencing power enhances people's
satisfaction with their friendships, romantic relationships, and jobs.

Exercise 1.5

Identify and relocate the disruptive text.

1. The size and orientation of an object affect, via pathways in visual and
   motor cortex, how people grasp it.
2. Unconscious thinking, for a range of problems, leads to better solutions.
3. People are quite skilled, despite remembering exact pitch inaccurately, at
   remembering patterns of changes in pitches.

Sometimes long sentences aren't clear because they sprawl. Despite a
solid core in which subject, verb, and object are linked well, the sentence
goes on and on. One clause is piled on top of another, almost as if the
author kept adding new thoughts while writing. Sentence 10a illustrates
sprawl:

(10a) People describe recent events concretely but distant events
abstractly, which is analogous to the description given near and far
objects, although individuals with depression are prone to abstract
descriptions regardless of spatial or temporal distance.

The sentence starts fine, with a story about how people describe recent
and distant events differently. But then it bogs down: One clause describes
similarities between descriptions of time and space and another describes
how descriptions differ when people are depressed.[1]

The first step in eliminating sentence sprawl is to remember the story line
and drop text that doesn't contribute. In sentence 10a, unless the work is

---

[1]By analogy, we can be grateful that the story of the three little pigs wasn't written
like this: "The third little pig built a house of bricks, which he bought at the local
home improvement center, although he could have paid less for the bricks online."

going to focus on the link between descriptions and depression, that clause could be deleted:

(10b) People describe recent events concretely but distant events abstractly, which is analogous to the description given near and far objects.

Sentence 10b is better but can be improved further. To see how, we need to explore some details of grammar. First, the clause beginning with *which* is a nonrestrictive or nondefining clause. It's not essential to the meaning of the sentence; 10b would be a complete sentence if it ended with *abstractly.* Instead, the nonrestrictive clause adds useful but not essential information. By contrast, in "The description that came first was concrete" *that came first* is a restrictive (defining) clause because it tells the reader which description was concrete (i.e., the one that came first).

Second, nonrestrictive clauses usually begin with *which.* This is a relative pronoun and, like any pronoun, needs an antecedent. In sentences such as 10b, the antecedent is often ambiguous. *Which* could refer to any of the words or phrases in the main clause (except *People*) or to the entire clause. Readers must figure this out for themselves, a process that delays their comprehension momentarily.

More often than not, *which* is a flag that a sentence is ending with a nonrestrictive clause that may sprawl. A trick for handling such sentences is to replace *which* with a word or phrase that provides a stronger connection between the sentence's main clause and the nonrestrictive clause.

(11a) Some hints about the impact of emotion on perception come from research on the attentional-blink paradigm, which shows that people identify emotionally significant words faster than neutral words.

In this sentence, the clause beginning with *which* is nonrestrictive (the sentence would be meaningful if it ended with *paradigm*), and you need to read that entire clause to know that the antecedent of *which* is *research.* We can replace *which* with a resumptive modifier, a key noun from the main clause. Because the nonrestrictive clause refers to *research*, that's a good choice to replace *which*:

(11b) Some hints about the impact of emotion on perception come from research on the attentional-blink paradigm, research showing that people identify emotionally significant words faster than neutral words.

In 11b, the clause leads with *research*, so the reader avoids the ambiguity of *which*. In other words, the repeated noun (*research*) anchors the clause, telling readers where they're headed. In the process, it avoids a sprawling sentence that seems to have no direction.

Sentences 12a and 12b illustrate the shortcomings of introducing a clause with *which* and the benefits of a resumptive modifier.

> (12a) Most prior studies of developmental change in processing speed have relied on samples of children living in the United States and Europe, which may bias conclusions about the shape of developmental functions.

> (12b) Most prior studies of developmental change in processing speed have relied on samples of children living in the United States and Europe, samples that may bias conclusions about the shape of developmental functions.

In 12b, I replaced *which* with *samples*. With this change, the reader immediately knows the topic of the nonrestrictive clause and the sentence no longer sprawls.

Sometimes the topic of the nonrestrictive clause is such that no single word from the main clause can be used to replace *which*. In this case, we use a word or phrase to summarize the relevant part of the main clause.

> (13a) Women who expect to encounter sexism are particularly attentive to words that are demeaning to females, which supports claims made by Allport (1954) more than 50 years ago.

In 13a, the nonrestrictive clause refers to the result that's described in the main clause; no noun from that clause can substitute for *which*. Instead, we can summarize that main clause by referring to it as *a result, a finding, an outcome*, or something similar:

> (13b) Women who expect to encounter sexism are particularly attentive to words that are demeaning to females, a finding that supports claims made by Allport (1954) more than 50 years ago.

Summative modifiers like this one function just as resumptive modifiers do: They replace a vague pronoun with a specific noun or noun phrase. In the process, summative modifiers reenergize a sentence, giving it direction.

Sentences 14a and 14b provide another example:

(14a) When people feel grateful to another person, they are more likely to reciprocate a favor, which tends to strengthen interpersonal relationships.

In this case, *which* refers to reciprocating a favor; *a behavior* or *an action* could be inserted instead:

(14b) When people feel grateful to another person, they are more likely to reciprocate a favor, a behavior that tends to strengthen interpersonal relationships.

Exercise 1.6

Use resumptive or summative modifiers to deal with sentence sprawl.

1. Male infants are more likely than female infants to recognize a familiar stimulus in a novel orientation, which is consistent with research showing that males excel at spatial tasks.

2. We tested participants on counting span, operation span, and reading span tasks, which are used to estimate working memory capacity.

3. Compared with high school students of the 1970s, today's high school students believe themselves to be more intelligent, which is further evidence for a trend of greater self-esteem in today's high school students.

Sentence sprawl can't be blamed entirely on nonrestrictive clauses that begin with *which*. Sometimes sentences sprawl when authors make comparisons or include lists. Sentence 15a illustrates sprawl from a comparison:

(15a) Studies with this paradigm typically find that people view members of their own group as friendly and kind but that out-group members are perceived to be hostile.

Sentence 16a shows sprawl from a list:

(16a) Motor vehicle accidents are a leading cause of deaths among adolescents because adolescents often exceed speed limits, driving is often done in conjunction with drinking alcohol, and seat belts are used rarely.

A good way to reduce the kind of sprawl seen in sentences 15a and 16a is by creating parallel structure—by expressing all the elements in the sentence in the same way, using the same grammatical forms. In sentence 15a, for example, the comparisons are completely inconsistent:

- one comparison involves active voice (*people . . . view members of their own group*) and another involves passive voice (*out-group members are perceived*);
- one comparison describes the target group completely (*members of their own group*), but the other uses a shorthand (*out-group members*); and
- one comparison mentions two traits (*friendly, kind*), but the other mentions only one (*hostile*).

By coordinating all of these comparisons—expressing them in the same terms—we get a sentence that isn't much shorter than 15a but avoids its sprawl:

(15b) Studies with this paradigm typically find that people view in-group members as friendly and kind but that they perceive out-group members as hostile and stingy.

Sentence 15b is easier to read because the comparisons are expressed using parallel structure: the voice is active, the groups are described with shorthand, and the number of traits is the same.

We could shorten it further by deleting *that they perceive*:

(15c) Studies with this paradigm typically find that people view in-group members as friendly and kind but out-group members as hostile and stingy.

And if you were really pressed for space, why not just use one trait per group?

(15d) Studies with this paradigm typically find that people view in-group members as friendly but out-group members as hostile.

We can use parallel structure to make sentence 16a flow better and be more concise. The trick with this sentence is to recast all of the properties (speeding, drinking, not wearing seatbelts) in terms of how teenagers drive:

> (16b)   Motor vehicle accidents are a leading cause of deaths among ado-lescents because adolescents often drive too fast, while drunk, and without wearing seatbelts.

Sometimes sprawl resists all of the techniques I've mentioned in the past few pages. In that case, there's no shame in splitting the long, sprawling sentence into two shorter, crisper sentences.

> (17a)   Risk-taking behavior is often thought to be a stable, pervasive per-sonality trait, but recent research suggests that it is specific to particular domains, such as sports, gambling, or investment, which explains why sky divers and bungee jumpers do not frequent casi-nos or play the stock market.

A summative modifier—replacing *which* with *a result that*—cuts the sprawl some but still leaves a mouthful:

> (17b)   Risk-taking behavior is often thought to be a stable, pervasive per-sonality trait, but recent research suggests that it is specific to particular domains, such as sports, gambling, or investment, a result that explains why sky divers and bungee jumpers do not frequent casinos or play the stock market.

It's time to bite the bullet and split the sentence in two:

> (17c)   Risk-taking behavior is often thought to be a stable, pervasive per-sonality trait, but recent research suggests that it is specific to particular domains, such as sports, gambling, or investment. This result explains why sky divers and bungee jumpers do not frequent casinos or play the stock market.

When you split a sentence in this manner, consider using a semicolon to separate it, like this:

> (17d)   Risk-taking behavior is often thought to be a stable, pervasive per-sonality trait, but recent research suggests that it is specific to particular domains, such as sports, gambling, or investment; this result explains why sky divers and bungee jumpers do not frequent casinos or play the stock market.

This is a subtle cue to the reader that the two independent clauses form a unit.

Exercise 1.7

Reduce the sprawl in these sentences by rewriting in parallel structure or as two sentences.

1. Among PhD-level scientists, those with greater SAT scores have more publications in scientific journals, and SAT score is positively correlated with the number of patents awarded.

2. For individuals who have approach goals in relationships, the number of positive features in the relationship predicts satisfaction with the relationship; when people have avoidance goals, relationship satisfaction is correlated with the absence of negative features in the relationship.

3. Research on the psychological correlates of human longevity shows that people with greater IQ scores tend to live longer, that greater conscientiousness is associated positively with longevity, and that the correlation between frequency of illness in childhood and age at death is negative.

WRAP UP

1. Eliminate nominalizations by revising sentences to put characters in the subject and actions in the verb.

2. Get to the subject quickly (avoid long introductory clauses) and don't interrupt the flow of subject-verb-object.

3. Avoid sentence sprawl by using resumptive and summative modifiers to begin nonrestrictive clauses and by describing comparisons and lists in parallel.

FOR PRACTICE

1. Search an article for nominalizations; replace the ones that you find.

2. Search for long introductory clauses; shorten or eliminate them.

3. Go on a *"which* hunt"—when you find one that's used to start a nonrestrictive clause, rewrite with a resumptive or summative modifier.

ANSWERS TO EXERCISES

Exercise 1.1

(1b) After a *return* from the site of physical *activity, consumption* of a sandwich, an apple, and a Diet Coke was accomplished by me.

(2a) The *demonstration* of contextual *influence* on visual *perception* is the primary *contribution* of this *report*.

(3a) *Overestimation* of negative *reactions* to unpleasant outcomes is common because of *underestimation* of *adjustment* to those outcomes.

Exercise 1.2

1. character = people; action = extracting the gist of a scene

    People extract the gist of a scene in a fraction of a second.[2]

2. character = our research; action = focus

    Our research focused on counterfactual reasoning.

3. character = East Asians and Westerners; action = disclosing personal information

    East Asians disclose personal information to friends less often than Westerners do.

Exercise 1.3

1. Interacting with nature replenishes directed-attention processes. OR

    When people interact with nature, their directed-attention processes are replenished.

2. When people feel clean, they judge others' moral transgressions less severely. OR

    People who feel clean judge others' moral transgressions less severely.

3. When processing lexical information, people are more accurate on consonants than vowels. OR

    People process consonants in lexical information more accurately than they process the vowels.

---

[2]The sentences I include as answers (here and throughout the book) are designed to illustrate possible answers. Please don't consider your answer "wrong" if it doesn't match mine word for word. Your sentence may be better than mine!

Exercise 1.4

1. Bilingual children have greater cognitive control than monolingual children because bilingual children have extensive experience selecting one language for production and inhibiting another. OR

   Compared with monolingual children, bilingual children have greater cognitive control because they have extensive experience selecting one language for production and inhibiting another.

2. During interracial interactions, white and black individuals experience anxiety but detect it only in members of their own race. OR

   Black and white individuals experience anxiety during interracial interactions but detect such anxiety only in members of their own race.

3. Given that experience helps infants learn words, we investigated the impact of experience on infants' mastery of syntax. OR

   We investigated the impact of experience on infants' mastery of syntax because prior work shows that experience helps infants segment words and associate names and shapes.

Exercise 1.5

1. Via pathways in visual and motor cortex, the size and orientation of an object affect how people grasp it. OR

   Pathways in visual and motor cortex convey information about the size and orientation of an object that affects how people grasp the object.

2. For a range of problems, unconscious thinking leads to better solutions. OR

   Unconscious thinking leads to better solutions for a range of problems.

3. Although people remember exact pitch inaccurately, they are quite skilled at remembering patterns of changes in pitches. OR

   People forget pitches, but they remember patterns of changes in pitches.

Exercise 1.6

1. Male infants are more likely than female infants to recognize a familiar stimulus in a novel orientation, a result consistent with research showing that males excel at spatial tasks. OR

   . . . novel orientation, a finding consistent with research showing . . .

2. We tested participants on counting span, operation span, and reading span tasks, tasks used to estimate working memory capacity. OR

   . . . reading span tasks, measures used to estimate . . .

3. Compared with high school students of the 1970s, today's high school students believe themselves to be more intelligent, an outcome that represents further evidence for a trend of greater self-esteem in today's high school students. OR

   . . . more intelligent, an observation that represents . . .

Exercise 1.7

1. Among PhD-level scientists, those with greater SAT scores have more publications in scientific journals and more patents. OR

   Among PhD-level scientists, greater SAT scores are correlated positively with more publications in scientific journals and more patents.

2. For individuals who have approach goals in relationships, the number of positive features in the relationship predicts satisfaction with the relationship; for individuals who have avoidance goals, the absence of negative features in the relationship predicts satisfaction. OR

   Relationship satisfaction is predicted by the number of positive features in the relationship for people who have approach goals but by the absence of negative features for people who have avoidance goals.

3. Research on the psychological correlates of human longevity shows that people who live longer tend to have greater IQ scores, to be more conscientious, and to have been ill less often during childhood. OR

   Research on human longevity shows that it tends to be correlated positively with IQ scores, with conscientious, and with good health during childhood.

Adding Emphasis

8

Kail, R. V.

Often you may want to emphasize an element of a text, such as a critical idea, an essential part of a procedure, or a key result. Novice writers sometimes convey emphasis with italic or bold fonts, but that practice is really an admission the author isn't confident that words alone will carry the message. In this lesson we'll consider two more effective ways to convey emphasis: through word choice and sentence structure.

Conveying Emphasis Through Word Choice

You can emphasize elements of a text by the words you use. Consider these two sentences—identical except for the italicized words:

(1a) The finding that parents *often* report greater happiness and greater life satisfaction than nonparents *is consistent with* the evolutionary claim that parenting satisfies basic human needs.

(1b) The finding that parents *consistently* report greater happiness and greater life satisfaction than nonparents *proves* the evolutionary claim that parenting satisfies basic human needs.

The second sentence seems more emphatic. Why? First, saying that "parents consistently report" describes a stronger finding than "parents often report." The former implies nearly all parents report greater happiness and satisfaction, but the latter implies only some do. Second, writing that these results "prove" the evolutionary claim is a much bolder statement than writing that the results are merely "consistent with" that claim.[1]

Words such as *consistently* and *prove* are intensifiers—they convey boldness, strength, and confidence. As in this example, adverbs are often used as intensifiers (*very, quite, certainly, always*) as are verbs (*show, prove, establish*) and adjectives (*key, crucial, essential, major*). Intensifiers function like the volume control on an amplifier, producing a "louder" text designed to ensure a reader doesn't miss a particularly important point.

---

[1]Many editors argue that *prove* is hardly ever warranted in psychological science, where conclusions are based on probabilistic evidence. They recommend that *prove* not be used; I agree.

Sometimes you may want to achieve the opposite effect: Instead of being bold and confident, you may want to be tentative and cautious. Hedges serve this function and come as adverbs (*often*, *sometimes*), adjectives (*many*, *some*), and verbs (*suggest*, *seems*). Sentence 1a has one hedge (*often*), and we could make the sentence sound even more cautious by inserting *seems*, as in sentence 1c:

> (1c) The finding that parents *often* report greater happiness and greater life satisfaction than nonparents *seems consistent with* the evolutionary claim that parenting satisfies basic human needs.

Sentence 2a begins with a neutral statement, and sentences 2b and 2c show the impact of adding an intensifier and hedge, respectively.

> (2a) Executive function predicts performance on analogical reasoning problems.

> (2b) Executive function *invariably* predicts performance on analogical reasoning problems.

> (2c) Executive function *occasionally* predicts performance on analogical reasoning problems.

Sentence 2b is bold, telling the reader that the link between executive function and analogical reasoning is ironclad. In contrast, sentence 2c is much softer, describing a weaker or fleeting link.

Exercise 2.1

Identify the hedges and intensifiers in these sentences.

1. Individuals who recognize emotions accurately tend to be more successful negotiators.

2. Unlike conservatives, liberals invariably view environmental issues in moral terms.

3. The principal influences on the ease with which children learn to read are letter-sound knowledge and phoneme awareness.

4. People typically judge threatening stimuli to be physically closer than they actually are.

Exercise 2.2

Revise these sentences twice, once by intensifying and once by hedging. Across the sentences, use a mix of verbs, adjectives, and adverbs.

1. People's posture expresses how powerful they feel.

2. Because better-educated people have more sophisticated decision-making skills and greater knowledge of health-related behavior, they are healthier than less-educated people.

3. Overhearing other people talk on cell phones is annoying because we only hear half of the conversation.

4. People who feel rejected and alienated are more aggressive verbally and physically.

You should choose intensifiers and hedges carefully. Writing that's filled with intensifiers can seem arrogant, a tone many readers find offensive. The three sentences in paragraph 3a are filled with intensifiers:

(3a) When people feel sad, they *invariably* think more deliberately. They have a *very* realistic view of their abilities and *never* rely on stereotypes. Consequently, these findings *prove* the old saying that "sadder is wiser."

Instead of respecting a reader's ability to reflect on a passage and draw reasonable conclusions, authors who write like this seem to be saying to a reader, "Open wide because I'm about to force a conclusion down your throat." So, use intensifiers carefully.

But writing that's replete with hedges is also ineffective. Here's the previous paragraph, with a hedge replacing each intensifier.

(3b) When people feel sad, they *sometimes* think more deliberately. They *may* have a realistic view of their abilities and *typically do not* rely on stereotypes. Consequently, these findings *appear to support* the old saying that "sadder is wiser."

Readers also react negatively to this version of the paragraph, but for different reasons. The reader thinks the author spineless—unwilling to state anything with confidence. And if the author lacks confidence in the writing, why should the reader trust the writing or, for that matter, even bother to read it?

These last two paragraphs underscore the importance of a proper balance between hedging and intensifying, of finding a voice that is neither arrogant not timid but instead cautiously confident. As you try to find this voice, one strategy is to start with a draft that includes no hedges or intensifiers; if they are stripped from paragraph 3b, we get this:

(3c) When people feel sad, they think more deliberately. They have a realistic view of their abilities and don't rely on stereotypes. Consequently, these findings support the old saying that "sadder is wiser."

You'll notice that without hedges or intensifiers, the paragraph seems reasonably confident. That's usually true: The absence of hedges typically produces a text that's fairly strong. (Notice that in this last sentence, I hedged three times!) Intensifiers should be added with care because they may change the tone from confident to arrogant. However, adding a hedge or two is often useful because it signals the reader that you've got faith in what you're writing but appreciate that the arguments may not be bullet-proof (e.g., a result may be open to another interpretation).

Exercise 2.3

Revise this paragraph twice, once in a cautious voice and again in a bold (but *not* a shove-it-down-your-throat) voice.

In Experiment 1, participants were more likely to remember a friend's birthday when that birthday was close to the participant's. In Experiment 2, participants learned more about a hypothetical person when that person's birthday was close to the participant's. These findings indicate that people are better able to remember information that is relevant to them personally.

Finally, avoid combining hedges and intensifiers in a way that sends a mixed message to your reader. For example, if you hedge your findings, it's best not to intensify the conclusions you draw from those findings. Be particularly careful to avoid combining hedges and intensifiers in the same sentence (e.g., "these findings definitely suggest" or "the results seem to demonstrate") as this will definitely confuse your readers. Probably.

Conveying Emphasis Through Sentence Structure

A politician giving a speech, a marathoner nearing the finish line, and a salesperson negotiating a deal all have something in common: They want to *end strong.* This same strategy works for conveying emphasis in your writing. You want to conclude a sentence strongly, saving the important, innovative, or provocative points for the end. For example, suppose you wanted to describe the emergence of a new theoretical framework. You might write the following:

(4a) A powerful theoretical framework for studying memory monitoring is suggested by these findings.

But there is greater emphasis on the theoretical framework if it comes at the end of the sentence:

(4b) These findings suggest a powerful theoretical framework for studying memory monitoring.

Now consider this pair of sentences:

(5a) Stable and substantial individual differences in working memory are shown in performance on N-back, complex span, and delayed matching-to-sample tasks.

(5b) Based on performance on N-back, complex span, and delayed matching-to-sample tasks, individual differences in working memory are stable and substantial.

Sentence 5a puts working-memory tasks at the end, and this position of emphasis leads one to anticipate that the author will be focusing on those tasks. In contrast, sentence 5b puts individual differences at the end, a change that leads the reader to expect more about the nature of those individual differences.

Let's look at some techniques for ending sentences with a bang, not a whimper.

Cut Unnecessary Material at the End of a Sentence

Consider this:

(6a) Individuals who have near-death experiences often renew their appreciation for life, with all of its ups and downs.

The important claim here is the link between near-death experiences and appreciation for life. Adding "with all of its ups and downs" contributes nothing because it simply mentions properties of life familiar to most readers. Eliminating that phrase puts the emphasis where it belongs, on renewed appreciation for life.

(6b) Individuals who have near-death experiences often renew their appreciation for life.

Here's another example:

(7a) When people are tired, their minds often wander from the task they are performing at the time.

This sentence is ineffective because the critical link—between fatigue and mind wandering—is obscured by the long description of the task. This is better:

(7b) When people are tired, their minds often wander from the task at hand.

And this might be better still:

(7c) When people are tired, their minds often wander.

Exercise 2.4

Trim unnecessary words to create greater emphasis.

1. When people are administered oxytocin, they are more cooperative with other people.

2. Among children who experience a natural disaster (e.g., Hurricane Katrina), those who view extensive TV coverage of the disaster often experience stress in their daily lives.

3. Multiple-choice tests do little to foster learning because the student need only recognize, not retrieve, the correct answer to the question.

Put Qualifying Material at the Beginning of a Sentence

Sometimes you may want to hedge a statement with a phrase. A common example is limiting the conditions under which a result typically occurs. For example, a finding may apply only to highly motivated participants or apply only to individuals living in poverty. Phrases that qualify a result work better at the beginning of a sentence than at the end. Look at the following pair of sentences:

(8a) Based on findings from the Add Health Study, individuals who have first sexual intercourse in early adolescence are more likely to be dissatisfied with their romantic relationships as adults.

(8b) Individuals who have first sexual intercourse in early adolescence are more likely to be dissatisfied with their romantic relationships as adults, based on findings from the Add Health Study.

The interesting finding here is the link between timing of first sexual intercourse and satisfying romantic relationships during adulthood. Sentence 8a emphasizes that result by placing it at the end of the sentence. In contrast, sentence 8b starts with the interesting result but ends weakly by specifying the source of the data producing the result.

The next pair of sentences shows the same pattern:

(9a) Based on studies of adults with mental illness and studies of ethnic minorities, individuals respond more positively to members of stig-matized groups after they have imagined interacting positively with members of those groups.

(9b) Individuals respond more positively to members of stigmatized groups after they have imagined interacting positively with mem-bers of those groups, based on studies of adults with mental ill-ness and studies of ethnic minorities.

Sentence 9a gets the qualifying information regarding methods out of the way and finishes strong by emphasizing a procedure to reduce hostility toward stigmatized groups. In contrast, sentence 9b leads with that interest-ing result but then takes the wind out of the story's sails by ending with a description of the kinds of studies that justify the conclusion.

There is an important exception to the rule of putting qualifying informa-tion at the beginning of a sentence: Sometimes the qualifying information is the information to be emphasized, which means it should appear at the end of the sentence, not the beginning. For example, sentence 8b might be preferred over sentence 8a if the idea being pursued is that the link between adolescent sex and relationship satisfaction is based solely on a single study and consequently needs to be replicated. Similarly, sentence 9b would work better than sentence 9a if the goal were to establish the need for research with additional stigmatized groups.

Exercise 2.5

Write two versions of a sentence that conveys this information, one in which the qualifying information is in the background and one in which it's essential.

Research shows that higher levels of the hormone oxytocin are associated with greater distress in interpersonal relationships. However, this relationship is found only for women, not men.

Move Important Elements Toward the End of the Sentence

Sometimes you want to move words toward the end of the sentence so they receive the emphasis they deserve. Here are two techniques to do this:

1. Insert *there/it/what* + a verb (usually a form of *to be*, such as *is*, *are*, *was*, or *were*):

Sentence 10a is clear but lacking in punch.

(10a) People more often cheat in a dimly lit room.

In 10a, the important ideas are distributed across the entire sentence: *People* is the subject's sentence, *cheat* is the verb, and the prepositional phrase *in a dimly lit room* ends the sentence. In contrast, 10b is strong because all these ideas are moved closer to the end of the sentence and united in an independent clause at the end of the sentence:

(10b) There is compelling evidence that people more often cheat in a dimly lit room.

Similarly, sentence 11a is clear but weak:

(11a) When humans look at a location where food is hidden, dogs look for the food in that spot.

But starting the sentence with "What is striking is that" puts the critical information closer to the end of the sentence:

(11b) What is striking is that when humans look at a location where food is hidden, dogs look for food in that spot.

Finally, sentence 12b uses "It is" to achieve greater emphasis:

(12a) Profiles on Facebook depict personality reasonably accurately.

(12b) It is noteworthy that profiles on Facebook depict personality reasonably accurately.

I suggest using these techniques sparingly, saving them for sentences that demand emphasis. Why? First, these techniques contradict the advice, from Lesson 1, that sentences have strong subjects and strong verbs. "It is" and "there are" are very weak (one reason why some teachers and editors suggest writers avoid them altogether). Second, they make sentences longer, which goes against the goal of writing concisely. Nevertheless, used occasionally, these techniques help to draw the reader's attention to a key point.

2. Add *not only X but Y*

One way to create emphasis is to contrast one element with others. For example, perhaps X is known to affect performance on a task; your work has shown that Y is an additional influence. The *not only X but Y* construction makes this comparison explicit and conveniently puts Y at the emphasis-receiving end of the sentence.

Suppose you've conducted a study on the impact of playing violent video games. You find that boys who play these games frequently are more aggressive and less engaged in school. The former result replicates previous studies, but the latter result is novel. You might write this:

(13a) Thus, adolescent boys who spend more time playing violent video games are more aggressive and less engaged in school.

This sentence is clear but does not highlight the novel result. Using *not only X but Y* makes the novel result stand out:

(13b) Thus, adolescent boys who spend more time playing violent video games are not only more aggressive but less engaged in school.

Similarly, if your novel claim is that ethical values influence consumer behavior, you might write this:

(14a) Consumers choose products based on price, quality, and a sense of social responsibility.

This is clear but does little to sell the novel idea.

(14b) Consumers choose products based not only on price and quality but on a sense of social responsibility.

Sentence 14b is more effective because *not only X but Y* contrasts the new idea with the accepted ideas.

Exercise 2.6

Use the four techniques I've just described to revise each of these sentences so the material to be emphasized is moved closer to the end of the sentence.

1. Individuals differ consistently in the emotions they feel most frequently and in the emotions they typically elicit in other people.

2. People are at greater risk for suicide when they have attempted suicide previously and when they have implicit thoughts about death.

3. For dogs and people, glucose boosts self-control.

4. When choosing a potential mate, humans consider features that can be assessed quickly because they are visible (e.g., height, weight) as well as features that require more time and effort to assess (e.g., education, occupation).

WRAP UP

1. Use intensifiers to add emphasis and hedges to convey caution. But don't overuse these words: Too many intensifiers make your writing seem arrogant and too many hedges make it seem feeble.

2. Put material you want to emphasize at the end of the sentence. Techniques for doing this include eliminating unnecessary words, putting qualifying comments at the beginning of a sentence, and shifting text to the right.

1. Identify hedges and intensifiers in a randomly selected paragraph; replace hedges with intensifiers and vice versa.

2. Find sentences that include unnecessary material at the end, material that causes them to end weakly.

3. Find sentences that put qualifying material in an introductory clause. Rewrite the sentences to have this material at the end; notice how the emphasis changes.

4. Find sentences that use *that/it/what* for emphasis. Delete this material and note the change in emphasis.

5. Find sentences that list multiple elements; revise using *not only X but Y* to emphasize one element.

ANSWERS TO EXERCISES

Exercise 2.1

1. Individuals who recognize emotions accurately *tend* [hedge] to be more successful negotiators.

2. Unlike conservatives, liberals *invariably* [intensifier] view environmental issues in moral terms.

3. The *principal* [intensifier] influences on the ease with which children learn to read are letter-sound knowledge and phoneme awareness.

4. People *typically* [hedge] judge threatening stimuli to be physically closer than they actually are.

Exercise 2.2

1. People's posture *seems to* express how powerful they feel. (hedge with verb)

   Everyone's posture expresses how powerful they feel. (intensify with adjective)

2. Because better-educated people *consistently* have more sophisticated decision-making skills and greater knowledge of health-related behavior, they are *inevitably* healthier than less-educated people. (intensify with adverbs)

Because better-educated people *often* have more sophisticated decision-making skills and greater knowledge of health-related behavior, they are *typically* healthier than less-educated people. (hedge with adverbs)

3. Overhearing other people talk on cell phones is *often* annoying because we only hear half of the conversation. (hedge with adverb)

   Overhearing other people talk on cell phones is *invariably* annoying because we only hear half of the conversation. (intensify with adverb)

4. *All* people who feel rejected and alienated are more aggressive verbally and physically. (intensify with adjective)

   People who feel rejected and alienated *tend to be* more aggressive verbally and physically. (hedge with verb)

Exercise 2.3

Cautious version:

In Experiment 1, *most* participants were more likely to remember a friend's birthday when that birthday was close to the participant's. In Experiment 2, participants *usually* learned more about a hypothetical person when that person's birthday was close to the participant's. These findings *suggest* that people *tend to be* better able to remember information that is relevant to them personally.

(I added an adjective in the first sentence, an adverb in the second, and some verbs in the third.)

Bold version:

In Experiment 1, participants *usually* remembered a friend's birthday when that birthday was close to the participant's. In Experiment 2, participants learned more about a hypothetical person when that person's birthday was close to the participant's. These findings *indicate* that people *consistently* remember information that is relevant to them personally.

(In the first sentence, I replaced *were more likely to remember* with the stronger *usually*. In the second sentence, I dropped *usually* but didn't add an intensifier. In the last sentence, I added a stronger verb and a strong adverb.)

Exercise 2.4

1. When people are administered oxytocin, they are more cooperative ~~with other people~~. (By definition, cooperation involves other people.)

2. Among children who experience a natural disaster (e.g., Hurricane Katrina), those who view extensive TV coverage of the disaster often experience stress ~~in their daily lives~~. (Where besides daily living can stress affect a person?)

3. Multiple-choice tests do little to foster learning because the student needs only recognize, not retrieve, the correct answer ~~to the question~~. (By definition, answers refer to questions.)

Exercise 2.5

Qualifying information in the background: For women but not men, higher levels of the hormone oxytocin are associated with greater distress in interpersonal relationships.

Qualifying information central: Higher levels of the hormone oxytocin are associated with greater distress in interpersonal relationships, but only for women and not men.

Exercise 2.6

1. It is striking that individuals differ consistently in the emotions they feel most frequently and in the emotions they typically elicit in other people. OR

   Individuals differ consistently not only in the emotions they feel most frequently but in the emotions they typically elicit in other people.

2. There is compelling evidence that people are at greater risk for suicide when they have attempted suicide previously and when they have implicit thoughts about death. OR

   It is noteworthy that people are at greater risk . . .

3. What emerges in this literature is that, for dogs and people, glucose boosts self-control. (To emphasize the similarity of the phenomenon across species, you could move the qualifying phrase to the end: What emerges in this literature is that glucose boosts self-control for dogs and people. Even better: What emerges in this literature is that glucose boosts self-control not only for people but for dogs.) OR

   There is abundant evidence that glucose boosts self-control in dogs and people.

4. When choosing a potential mate, humans consider not only features that can be assessed quickly because they are visible (e.g., height,

weight) but features that require more time and effort to assess (e.g., education, occupation). OR

What is noteworthy is that when humans choose a potential mate, they consider features that can be assessed quickly because they are visible (e.g., height, weight) and features that require more time and effort to assess (e.g., education, occupation).

Writing Concisely with Some Spice

Kail, R. V.

Confession time: This lesson is actually two mini-lessons, one about writing concisely and one about adding spice to your writing. Neither topic warrants a full lesson, which is why I've merged them here. We start with writing concisely.

Writing Concisely

Scientific writing is concise. Why? One reason is that scientists are busy and can't waste time reading wordy reports. A second reason is that many journals limit the number of words they will accept in a manuscript (e.g., 2,500 words for a research report in *Psychological Science*). A third reason—my favorite—is that it's aesthetically satisfying to hit the "sweet spot" on length—just the right number of words for readers to understand a study fully, no more, no less.

In this half lesson, I mention four tips for concise writing.

Change Negatives to Affirmatives

Most phrases of the form *not + X* can be rewritten in the affirmative:

$$\text{not missing} \rightarrow \text{present}$$
$$\text{not stop} \rightarrow \text{continue}$$
$$\text{not empty} \rightarrow \text{full}$$

Sentence 1a includes such a *not + X* phrase:

(1a) Salespeople more often invest extra effort when a customer is not rude.

If the *not + X* is replaced,

(1b) Salespeople more often invest extra effort when a customer is polite.

we use one fewer word. Just as important, the sentence becomes slightly clearer because definitions involving the absence of features (e.g., *not rude*) are typically vaguer than those involving the presence of features (e.g., *polite*). In other words, definitions are more precise when they specify what something is rather than what it is not.

Exercise 3.1

Change the negatives to affirmatives.

1. There are not many studies on the impact of color on memory for scenes.
2. People sometimes do not remember the source of their memories.
3. Exposure to alcohol ads has behavioral consequences that do not differ from those obtained from actually consuming alcohol.

Delete What Readers Can Infer

Writers sometimes include adjectives that are redundant; they're unnecessary because they're implicit in the noun they modify. Examples include *terrible tragedy, true facts, and future plans.* By definition, tragedies are terrible, facts are true, and plans are for the future. The adjectives are wasted words. Consequently, in this sentence

(2a) After participants had completed the experiment, they were given a free gift.

we can delete *free* without any loss in meaning because by definition gifts are free:

(2b) After participants had completed the experiment, they were given a gift.

Similarly, many adverbs are unnecessary because they're implicit in the verbs they modify. Examples here include *finish completely, prove conclusively*, and *suggest tentatively.*

A related mistake is to include categories that are implied by words. Examples include *period of time, red in color, triangular in shape, heavy in weight*, and *depreciate in value.* In each of these cases, the category (e.g., time, color, shape) is implied by the initial noun, adjective, or verb. In sentence 3a, for example,

(3a) All the participants were of the male gender.

gender is unnecessary because it's implicit in *male*:

(3b) All the participants were male.

This tip, like the previous one, only saves a word or two. But these can add up over the course of a manuscript.

Exercise 3.2

Delete what readers can infer.

1. What's particularly striking is that the effect of misperception on inter-group conflict was large in size.

2. After participants had completely finished the perspective-taking task, they were tested on a working-memory task.

3. When people believe that free will is an illusion, they are more likely to behave in ways that are deceitful in nature.

Replace Phrases With Words

English is filled with short phrases that can be replaced with a single word. Table 3.1 lists some illustrative examples, but there are hundreds more!

Table 3.1   Common Phrases That Can Be Replaced by a Single Word

Phrase	Word
A large percentage of	Most
As a consequence of	Because
At that point in time	Then
At the present time	Now
Due to the fact that	Because
In close proximity to	Near
In some cases	Sometimes
In the near future	Soon
In the situation where	When
Subsequent to	After
With the exception of	Except

For example, in sentence 4a

(4a) In the event that synesthesia is a product of learning, pairing of sounds and visual symbols reflects a person's experiences.

In the event that can be replaced by *if*—saving three words (and 15 characters!).

(4b) If synesthesia is a product of learning, pairing of sounds and visual symbols reflects a person's experiences.

Because English has so many phrases like those in Table 3.1, you can't hope to remember them all. Instead, as you edit your writing, pay attention to sets of words that gain their meaning from being together. Then see if you can replace them with a single word.

Exercise 3.3

Identify phrases that can be replaced by an individual word.

1. Participants were told to determine the location of the target in an array of photographs.
2. Emotionally significant words have a tendency to be identified more accurately than emotionally neutral words.
3. During the time that participants in the control group were sitting, those in the experimental group were jogging.

Delete Adverbs and Adjectives

This may seem like a radical proposal—eliminating two parts of speech! However, too many writers insert adjectives or adverbs that have little meaning. Consequently, a good revision strategy is to create a version of a sentence with no adjectives or adverbs and then reinsert only those essential to the sentence's meaning.

In sentence 5a, the adjectives and adverbs are in italics; in sentence 5b, they've been deleted.

(5a) Interviewers *often* gesture during *routine investigative* interviews, a *nonverbal* behavior that *certainly* affects the interviewee's *vocal* responses.

(5b) Interviewers gesture during interviews, a behavior that affects the interviewee's responses.

One approach is to rank the deleted words in their importance to the sentence. (Of course, the surrounding sentences provide a context that determines the importance of individual words; not knowing that context, our choices are more tentative.) Of the six italicized words (*often, routine, investigative, nonverbal, certainly, vocal*), I would rank *investigative* as the most important; it seems essential because it identifies the setting in which gestures take place. I would rank *routine* and *certainly* as the least important. How does a routine investigative interview differ from one that's nonroutine? *Certainly* is an intensifier that's unnecessary: *behavior that affects the interviewee's responses* is sufficiently strong. *Often* is a hedge; it could be included if the authors want to be cautious regarding their claims. *Nonverbal* and *vocal* might be important if the context emphasized the contrast between different modes of communicative behavior; otherwise, they could remain deleted. My preferred version of the sentence is this:

(5c) Interviewers *often* gesture during *investigative* interviews, a behavior that affects the interviewee's responses.

Sentence 6a provides another example in which adjectives and adverbs are italicized; in sentence 6b, they've been omitted.

(6a) Following a violation of *human* trust, a *sincere* apology repairs trust only when people *really* believe that *moral* character is *actually* *malleable*.

(6b) Following a violation of trust, an apology repairs trust only when people believe that character is malleable.

Of the six deleted words—*human, sincere, really, moral, actually, malleable*—two seem essential: *moral* and *malleable*. Both are at the heart of the story; apologies "work" when people believe a person's moral nature can be changed. But none of the rest seems essential: *trust* is usually between people, and the rest of the sentence makes it clear that this story is about human trust. Unless indicated to the contrary, apologies are assumed to be *sincere*, and *really* and *actually* add nothing (e.g., *is actually malleable = is malleable*). Sentence 6c is the version I prefer:

(6c) Following a violation of trust, an apology repairs trust only when people believe that *moral* character is *malleable*.

This delete-all-adjectives-and-adverbs strategy is labor intensive but worth the effort: In both examples, four words were deleted, producing sentences that were not only shorter but crisper. Until this leaner style of writing comes naturally, one step of your revising might be to delete one adjective (or adverb) from every sentence or five from each paragraph. For some sentences and paragraphs this won't be possible. But most of the time you'll find plenty of excess adjectives and adverbs, a process that will hone your skill in identifying nonessential words. And used with the other strategies mentioned here (change negatives to affirmatives, delete what readers can infer, replace phrases with words), your writing will get closer to that aesthetically pleasing sweet spot on length.

Exercise 3.4

Identify all the adjectives and adverbs; delete those that are unnecessary.

1. Married individuals who verbally report having a truly happy marriage actually have better physical health and increased longevity.

2. The testing effect refers to the psychological phenomenon that repeated retrieval of information actually helps people to remember that same information much better.

3. When people listen carefully to extremely sad music, they are relatively biased to hear many words that relate to death.

Adding Spice

I've searched the Internet high and low but can't find a single website that says scientific writing should be boring. Nevertheless, many writers seem to strive for a style that's clear but so dull that *How to Repair Your Lawnmower* seems riveting by comparison. This is silly; science is not well served when articles make for tedious reading. Science is exciting, and there's no reason why articles shouldn't convey that excitement to the reader. In this mini-lesson, I suggest several tips for spicing up your scientific writing. They won't turn you into a bestselling novelist, but they will help to create a story line that's lively and engaging.

Active Writing

In the lesson on writing clearly, I emphasized that sentences are easier to understand when they have characters as subjects and the characters' actions as verbs. That practice also makes your writing more animated and more appealing. As a reminder of the pitfalls of sentences filled with nominalizations, sentence 7a

> (7a) Income inequality at the national level is negatively correlated with happiness.

is no more engaging than a repair manual. But revised to emphasize characters and actions,

> (7b) People are relatively happy when their country's wealth is distributed evenly.

the sentence comes alive; it's no longer about abstractions but what makes people happy.

Figures of Speech

Skilled writers often enrich their prose with figures of speech—devices in which words are used in special ways to achieve a distinct effect. For example, in hyperbole exaggerated statements are used for emphasis. In understatement, the description is deliberately less strong than the facts or conditions warrant. Frankly, both hyperbole and understatement are risky for scientific writing because of the possibility that readers will interpret them literally, not figuratively.

Simile and Metaphor

Other figures of speech are more useful. Simile and metaphor both involve comparing dissimilar objects, typically so the text is clearer or more vivid. In other words, similes and metaphors can aid comprehension by comparing a novel idea or concept with familiar ideas or concepts. For example, sentence 8 refers to the familiar Nike swoosh to indicate the reliable signs of ADHD.

> (8) Hyperactivity, inattention, and impulsivity signify ADHD, just as the swoosh signifies Nike products.

Similarly, sentence 9 uses grammar to introduce a system for combining goal-directed actions:

(9) Just as grammar specifies legal combinations of words, means-end parse indicates how actions can be combined to achieve goals.

In addition to aiding comprehension, simile and metaphor can make sentences more vivid. They are often handy for emphasizing size-related phenomena, such as the strength of an effect, the likelihood an event will occur, or the (relative) ease of a task. Sentence 10 uses a simile to express how easily a target was detected:

(10) The misoriented letter was detected as readily as a red cap on a field of new-fallen snow.

Sentence 11 uses a metaphor to emphasize that an effect was large:

(11) The difference in change detection in the face and house conditions represents an industrial-strength effect.

Finally, sentence 12 uses a simile to emphasize that a phenomenon is likely:

(12) In short, adolescents who are self-conscious in the presence of peers are as common as ants at a summer picnic.

Of course, metaphors and similes aren't restricted to size-related comparisons; most ideas can be made more familiar and more interesting with simile and metaphor. You can find scores of websites devoted to metaphors and similes that can inspire you to create your own. As you do, however, be wary of three traps that can snare a novice metaphor writer. (Notice that metaphor?) First, avoid mixed metaphors like the one in sentence 13a.

(13a) Readers were flying high with congruous text but drowning with incongruous text.

The problem is that the sentence begins with a comparison to flying and then shifts to a comparison with swimming. Sentence 13b eliminates this problem by having a constant reference: smooth and difficult sailing.

(13b) Readers had smooth sailing with congruous text but encountered choppy water with incongruous text.

However, sentence 13b illustrates a second trap: a cliché. Hundreds (thousands?) of writers have used this comparison (smooth vs. choppy waters) before, which makes it less vivid. Sentence 14a has the same problem:

(14a) Thus, when walking on unsteady surfaces, infants are slower than snails.

Sentence 14b avoids the clichéd comparison:

(14b) Thus, when walking on unsteady surfaces, infants are slower than a checkout line at Best Buy on Black Friday.

Nevertheless, sentence 14b illustrates a third trap: Similes and metaphors are effective only when readers understand the reference—in this case that a checkout line at Best Buy on Black Friday often moves very, very slowly. Readers who aren't familiar with Black Friday[1] (or don't know that Best Buy is a chain of electronics stores) will end up confused, not enlightened.

These examples show that the road to a successful metaphor is filled with obstacles. But the effort is worth it because reaching that destination can animate your writing and make it stand out from ordinary scientific text.

Exercise 3.5

Complete the sentence with a simile or metaphor. The words in brackets hint at a basis of comparison.

1. Speed of information processing increases steadily in childhood and adolescence, as if . . . [upgrading a computer's CPU].

2. When individuals with Parkinson's disease reach for an object, their hand moves a short distance, slows, and then moves again in a different direction like . . . [ship navigator].

3. According to ego-depletion theories, self-control depends on a limited pool of mental resources, just as . . . [muscle movements].

---

[1]Black Friday is the Friday after the American Thanksgiving holiday and marks the start of the Christmas shopping season in the United States. Stores are usually packed with shoppers looking for good deals.

Antimetabole

You probably don't know another useful figure of speech by name, but you'll recognize familiar examples, all from U.S. presidents:

(15) What counts isn't necessarily the size of the *dog* in the *fight*—it's the size of the *fight* in the *dog*. (Eisenhower)

(16) Ask not what *your country* can do for *you*; ask what *you* can do for *your country*. (Kennedy)

(17) *America* did not invent *human rights* . . . *Human rights* invented *America*. (Carter)

These examples illustrate antimetabole, a figure of speech in which words are repeated, in reverse order. Sentences 15 through 17 illustrate several properties of antimetabole:

- The repeated words are often nouns or noun phrases.
- The nouns are usually linked by the same word (or words) in both instances.
- The nouns usually appear in a later phrase or clause of the same sentence.

A first step in creating your own antimetabole is to identify two nouns that refer to key elements in your work. Then think about verbs or phrases that describe how these elements are related in your work. As an example, consider research on people's religious beliefs. This literature demonstrates wide-ranging behavioral consequences of belief in God but has done little to clarify the nature of those beliefs. I chose *God* and *belief* as the key nouns and after some experimentation came up with this:

(18) Thus, research reveals much about the impact of *people's belief* in *God* but tells little about the *God* in *people's beliefs*.

As another example, sentence 19 summarizes findings that show mutual influence of emotional control on the quality of marriage:

(19) In other words, couples who frequently *control their emotions for the sake of their marriage* sometimes end up *controlling their marriage for the sake of their emotions*.

Creating good antimetaboles is challenging, but they can be remarkably effective, especially as the last sentence of a paper. It's not a coincidence that sentences with antimetabole rank high among the best-known quotations of historical figures.

Exercise 3.6

Finish the sentence with an antimetabole that uses the italicized words and describes the findings in brackets.

1. *Neglecting your siblings* will lead . . . [siblings will ignore you].

2. When teams *lose sight of outcomes*, the likely . . . [they probably won't win].

3. People do not *know* how much others *remember* but . . . [other people's knowledge is something they do retain].

Creating New Words

Many fiction writers create new words specifically to enliven their storytelling. Shakespeare was an expert, creating more than 1,000 new words (and we can thank him for the always useful *puke*), and modern novelists such as J. K. Rowling continue the practice (Plotnik, 2007). Used sparingly and carefully, such neologisms can enhance scientific writing, too.

There are many techniques for creating new words, including shortening an existing word (e.g., *prob* for *probably*, *obv* for *obviously*), blending existing words (e.g., *snowmageddon* to refer to a massive snowstorm, *Brangelina* to refer to Brad Pitt and Angelina Jolie), and using the names of well-known people as nouns or verbs (e.g., *Tebowing* to mean dropping to a knee to pray). Here I focus on three other options because they seem the easiest to use and work well with psychological content.

Adding Prefixes and Suffixes

English is filled with prefixes and suffixes; Table 3.2 lists some familiar examples. Adding one of them to an existing word is the simplest way to create a new word. For example, a meaning that is readily conveyed by gesture is *gesturable*; individuals who thrive on excluding others from social interactions are *excludaholics*.

Table 3.2 Common Prefixes and Suffixes That Can Be Used to Create New Words

Prefix	Meaning	Suffix	Meaning
a (an)-	without	-able	capable of
macro/micro-	large/small	-aholic	one addicted to something
mis-	faulty	-cian/-ee/-er	one who
neo-	new	-ism	belief system
omni-	all, always	-ize	to cause
pseudo-	fake, false	-ness	state of

Exercise 3.7

Combine the italicized word with a prefix or suffix from Table 3.2 to make a new word that fits the definition given in each sentence.

1. A facial expression that looks like a *smile* but isn't because it doesn't engage muscles in the mouth and eyes.
2. A pattern of *transfer* in which original learning extends to nearly all novel tasks.
3. *Retrieval* that is inaccurate because it yields stimuli similar to those presented instead of those that were actually presented.

Hyperhyphenated Modifiers

English is filled with hyphenated phrases that work as a unit to modify a word, typically a noun. Familiar examples include a *deer-in-the-headlights* look, a *state-of-the-art* computer, and an *over-the-top* experience. But you can create your own hyphenated phrases, as I did on page 20 in suggesting that you avoid a *shove-it-down-your-throat* voice. Some other examples include *choke-under-pressure* leaders, *aggressive-toward-other-people* dreams, and *faster-reaction-times-are-associated-with-reduced-mortality* effects.

A common situation where hyperhyphenation is useful is a sentence with a long noun phrase, such as sentence 20a:

(20a) The finding that memory was superior for the location of taboo words supports . . .

This sentence is difficult because readers must slog through a long phrase before they get to the main verb: 10 words separate the subject, *finding*, from the verb, *supports*. Using hyperhyphenation produces this:

(20b)   The superior-memory-for-location-of-taboo-words finding supports . . .

Hyperhyphenation cues the reader that the words should be a unit. Placing them before the noun (as we would with any adjective) puts the subject and verb of the sentence together. But the main reason for hyperhyphenation is that its very novelty (particularly in scientific writing) highlights the hyphenated words and, in the process, adds some zip to your text.

Before you go wild with hyperhyphenation, some warnings. First, don't use a hyperhyphenated phrase when an existing adjective would fit perfectly. If you write *have-abundant-material-possessions people* instead of *affluent people*, readers will think that either your vocabulary is limited or you're showing off. Second, be particularly careful when using hyperhyphenated phrases to describe people because this can be dehumanizing (i.e., it equates the person with the description and makes the person nothing more than a group member). In other words, people with many material possessions are not just wealthy; they may also be friendly, happy, or irresponsible. Referring to them as *affluent people* reduces them to a single dimension and makes the group seem more homogeneous than it is. Third, avoid *Hey!-look-what-I-can-do-with-lots-of-hyphens-in-my-writing-to-get-your-undivided-attention* phrases. As a rule of thumb, hyperhyphenated phrases are probably most effective when they include three to five words.

Exercise 3.8

Hyperhyphenate to create a phrase that modifies the italicized noun.

1. The *motive* to perceive the social system as fair is particularly well established . . .

2. The findings help to explain the prevalence of *people* who see the forest before the trees.

3. *People* performing better in the morning illustrates . . .

Verbing

Fifty years ago, *dialogue, impact,* and *message* were used only as nouns, but today it's common to hear each used as a verb.

(21) Effective bosses frequently *dialogue* with their employees.

(22) Learning a second language during childhood can *impact* the development of executive control.

(23) Western adolescents often *message* their feelings rather than showing them overtly.

Such verbing is most effective when the meaning of the new verb is novel and obvious. The well-known *google* fits these criteria. So does *podium,* as in *The relay team hopes to podium in the upcoming Olympic games.*

To do your own verbing, search for nouns. You'll discover that many don't qualify because they already have verb forms. (Remember, this is how nominalizations are created, by making a noun from a verb or adjective.) Good candidates are often nouns that serve as objects of verbs. For example, in sentence 24a

(24a) Strangers often achieve *rapport* when their body movements are coordinated.

rapport is the object of *achieve.* In sentence 24b, it's now a brand-new verb:

(24b) Strangers often *rapport* when their body movements are coordinated.

Similarly, in sentence 25a

(25a) Pursuing a *goal* often happens unconsciously.

goal is the object of *pursuing.* In sentence 25b, it's become a verb:

(25b) *Goaling* often happens unconsciously.

As you pursue verbing, two words of caution. First, be sure that the new verb captures the meaning of the words it's replacing. For example, in my first attempts to write this section, I thought *gist* was a good candidate for verbing, as shown in the following pair of sentences:

(26a) Adults readily recall the *gist* of stories.

(26b) Adults *gist* stories.

In fact, *gist* didn't work well as a verb because *gist stories* does not necessarily imply *recall the gist of stories*. It might mean that adults readily perceive the gist of stories or refer to other actions people might perform on *gist*.

Second, as was true for words created from prefixes and suffixes, verbed words are best used after the context establishes their meaning, such as at the end of an Introduction or Discussion section. And I recommend you create no more than one or two new words per paper. With one (or two) new words, readers are likely to enjoy the novelty and appreciate the descriptive power of the new word. With more than two new words, readers will find you guilty of way-over-the-top writing.

Exercise 3.9

Enliven these sentences by making the italicized word a verb.

1. These findings suggest that parents are rarely successful when they try to make their shy children more *extroverted.*
2. Contact with *nature* makes people feel happy.
3. People who violate *taboos* (e.g., they cheat or steal) often are punished for their behavior.

WRAP UP

1. Make your writing more concise by changing negatives to affirmatives, deleting what readers can infer, replacing phrases with words, and including only essential adjectives and adverbs.

2. Make your writing livelier by writing actively, relying on figures of speech (simile, metaphor, antimetabole), and creating new words.

FOR PRACTICE

1. Search for negatives and replace with affirmatives, replace phrases with words, and decide which adjectives and adverbs are unnecessary.

2. In an Introduction or Discussion section, clarify a complex idea with a simile or metaphor.

3. In the last paragraph of a Discussion, create a final sentence that includes antimetabole.

4. In an Introduction or Discussion section, create new words by adding a prefix or suffix, using hyperhyphenation, or verbing.

ANSWERS TO EXERCISES

Exercise 3.1

1. There are *few* studies on the impact of color on memory for scenes.

2. People sometimes *forget* the source of their memories.

3. Exposure to alcohol ads has behavioral consequences that *are similar to* those obtained from actually consuming alcohol.

Exercise 3.2

1. What's particularly striking is that the effect of misperception on intergroup conflict was large ~~in size~~.

2. After participants had ~~completely~~ finished the perspective-taking task, they were tested on a working-memory task.

3. When people believe that free will is an illusion, they are more likely to behave in ways that are deceitful ~~in nature~~.

Exercise 3.3

1. Participants were told to ~~determine the location of~~ *find* the target in an array of photographs.

2. Emotionally significant words ~~have a tendency~~ *tend* to be identified more accurately than emotionally neutral words.

3. ~~During the time that~~ *While* participants in the control group were sitting, those in the experimental group were jogging.

Exercise 3.4

Adjectives and adverbs are in italics.

1. *Married* individuals who *verbally* report having a *truly happy* marriage *actually* have *better physical* health and *increased* longevity.

   Individuals who report having a *happy* marriage have *better physical* health and *increased* longevity.

2. The *testing* effect refers to the *psychological* phenomenon that *repeated* retrieval of information *actually* helps people to remember that *same* information *much* better.

    The *testing* effect refers to the phenomenon that *repeated* retrieval of information helps people to remember that information better.

3. When people listen *carefully* to *extremely sad* music, they are *relatively* biased to hear *many* words that relate to death.

    When people listen to *sad* music, they are biased to hear words that relate to death.

Exercise 3.5

1. Speed of information processing increases steadily in childhood and adolescence, as if the child's mental hardware is constantly being upgraded to a newer, faster CPU.

2. When individuals with Parkinson's disease reach for an object, their hand moves a short distance, slows, and then moves again in a different direction like a ship directed by an unskilled navigator.

3. According to ego-depletion theories, self-control depends on a limited pool of mental resources, just as movements of muscles draw from a limited supply of glucose.

Exercise 3.6

1. Neglecting your siblings will lead your siblings to neglect you.

2. When teams lose sight of outcomes, the likely outcome is to lose.

3. People do not know how much others remember but they do remember how much others know.

Exercise 3.7

1. pseudosmile

2. omnitransfer

3. misretrieval

Exercise 3.8

1. The *perceive-the-social-system-as-fair* motive is particularly well established . . .

2. The findings help to explain the prevalence of *see-the-forest-before-the-trees* people.

3. *Performing-better-in-the-morning* people illustrate . . .

Exercise 3.9

1. These findings suggest that parents are rarely successful when they try to *extrovert* their shy children.

2. *Naturing* makes people feel happy.

3. People who *taboo* (e.g., they cheat or steal) often are punished for their behavior.

Writing the Discussion Chapter

Harrison, E. and Rentzelas, P.

The final chapter of the dissertation document is the discussion chapter. This is where you summarise and discuss your findings in relation to previous literature, your hypotheses and research aims, your theoretical perspective, future research, and practical applications. The discussion really gives you the opportunity to showcase your academic skills, to demonstrate your understanding of the topic area, of your empirical findings, and of the theory behind your project. The discussion is the only part of the dissertation that you will not receive any formative feedback on, and so it is also the most independent piece of the whole dissertation. It is also one of the most important sections of the dissertation as it summarises your findings and concludes the 'story' behind your project.

There are 7 key parts that make up a good discussion chapter:

1. Summarise your findings
2. Relate your findings to your hypothesis/es and previous literature
3. Attempt to explain why you got the findings you did
4. Discuss the limitations of your methodology/project
5. Discuss directions for future research
6. Revisit the unique contribution of your project
7. Consider the practical applications of your findings

Let's consider each of these in turn:

1. Summarise your findings
The first section of the discussion chapter should be a summary of your findings. You shouldn't use statistics here; try instead to explain what you have found using words. Remember that by this point your reader will have read your introduction, so they will know what your research questions are. They will also have read your methodology, so they know how you have addressed your research questions. They will also have read your results, so they know roughly what you have found. Now you need to give your account of how the research questions have been answered. So in this section what we really want to see is a summary of what the findings are.

2. Relate your findings to the literature and your hypothesis/es
Once you have summarised your findings, you should think about how your findings relate to the literature you have discussed in the literature review. Did your findings support previous

literature in the area? Also consider your hypothesis or hypotheses, and whether the data support or refute what you predicted. If you are conducting qualitative research, you will not have a hypothesis, but you can still discuss the relationship with the literature. If you had multiple aims or research questions, it may be worth breaking this section down to discuss each question in turn. The main purpose of this section is to account for your findings in relation to literature and consider whether your findings were expected or not.

Don't worry if your findings didn't support your hypothesis or the literature – this does not mean that you won't be able to produce a good discussion chapter. If this happens, your next job is to explain why this might have happened, and what the reasons are for getting the results you did.

3. Explain your findings

As well as summarising your main findings, it is important to also be able to explain why your findings occurred. It's important to consider your theoretical perspective here, explaining why you believe you obtained the results you did. Consider why and how two particular variables might be related, why two groups of individuals might perform differently on a particular task, or why discussing a particular topic might give rise to particular themes. Regardless of your design or research questions, the key word here is "why?"

4. Discuss the limitations of your methodology

Even though your theoretical perspective might provide a perfectly good explanation for why certain findings might have occurred, there will always be limitations which could have had an influence on the findings, and there will always be some parts of the research project that could benefit from improvement if the study were to be replicated. You should refer to these as limitations, not weaknesses. Weaknesses in a design suggest that you didn't fully think through the design before conducting it, whereas limitations imply things that were relatively uncontrollable, such as access to participants and specific materials.

When you discuss the limitations of your study, you should make sure that you fully explain each of your points, elaborating on how each of these limitations could have influenced your findings. For example, if your sample was from a student population within a particular institution, you may conclude that the sample was not representative of a wider population. However, you need to also make sure you discuss the reasons why a different sample may have produced different results, thus explaining your theoretical perspective on the sample used. You may also conclude that the sample size was small, probably due to the time restraints of the dissertation. However, you should be wary of making statements such as this, as the module has been designed to allow you time to conduct a scientific project. Claiming that you ran out of time could therefore imply that you did not manage your time effectively.

5. Discuss directions for future research

Once you have discussed and explained your findings and the limitations of your research, you should now consider how future research could build upon your work. Think of research as a *journey*. You started with what was already out there, found a gap (or gaps) and tried to fill these gaps with your project. Now that you have completed your project, further doors will open to new research ideas. Perhaps you could focus on a different population, or alter the methodology to use more reliable tasks? Perhaps you could alter your hypothesis, or the focus of your research questions? Try to be creative here, rather than just addressing the limitations you have discussed above.

6. Revisit the unique contribution of your project

The unique contribution of your project should have been highlighted in the rationale at the end of the literature review. At this point in the discussion, you should reconsider this, and discuss where your project has succeeded. Despite the limitations of your project, what contribution can your study make to the research literature and knowledge in the area? Taking your findings into consideration, what do we know now that we didn't know before? This is your chance to really sell your project to your readers and clarify the unique contribution that you have made by conducting this piece of research.

7. The practical applications

Finally, you should consider how your findings could have an impact in the real world, and how the results of your study can be applied in research, knowledge or practice. For example, there may be implications for the medical profession, counselling, or the NHS if you have conducted a clinical-type study or a qualitative interview. There may be implications for practice in schools, or to knowledge of development and education if you have conducted a school-based project. There may be applications to applied areas of psychology, such as health, neurology, cognition, development, social, education, or sport. You should try to consider how your findings can impact our understanding of the topic area, too, as this helps to emphasise the uniqueness of your project and adds to the selling point of your research.

Putting Together the Final Dissertation

Harrison, E. and Rentzelas, P.

If you are reading this section it means that you are on the final stages of your dissertation project. Well done! At this stage we need to make sure that you know how to put together all the different sections of your dissertation and that you respond to the formative feedback that you have received from your supervisor. The aim of this chapter is go over the main questions that students devour when they have reached the final stage of the dissertation and to highlight some of the most common editing mistakes that students make.

Key issues and common mistakes with formatting
The most common mistakes that students make when they are formatting their final dissertation document are APA errors, including (but not exclusive) to the following:

- Citations not in alphabetical order
- Indents not used (main body or ref. list)
- Apostrophes used for quotations

  o Use "quotation marks"
  o Apostrophes used to emphasise a point

- Use of *italics*
- Repeated "openers" to sentences
- Bad grammar

Your final dissertation should be font size 12, *only* in Times New Roman, and margins 2.54 cm at the top, right and bottom, and 3 cm on the left. The spacing between lines should be 1.5 or double. Furthermore, remember that first line is indent for *all* main text paragraphs. Please see the example bellow:

> Prejudice is "...an unjustified negative attitude toward an individual based solely on that individual's membership in a group" (Worchel, Cooper, & Goelthal, 1988, p.449). However, as Fiske (2000) states"...thoughts and feelings do not exclude, oppress, and kill people; behavior does" (p.312). Thus, discrimination, defined as a means of "...limit[ing] or restrict[ing] access to privileges or resources by a minority group" (Stratton & Hayes, 1999, p.79) warrants closer investigation if social psychologists wish to make a useful contribution to reducing prejudice.

Research establishing a relation between prejudice and discrimination is somewhat mixed. Some early research indicates a dissociation between the attitude of prejudice and

What do you need to include with your dissertation?

The following list details the sections that need to be included in the final dissertation and the order of presentation. Remember that you can only submit one item to the submission portal, so all of the following needs to be in a single document.

- **Assessment cover sheet –** will be uploaded to Moodle
- **Title page –** APA format
- **Authors declaration page –** on Moodle (signed)
- **Acknowledgments –** optional.
- **Abstract –** 150–250 words (although this does not count towards the word count of the final dissertation, the length of the abstract needs to comply with APA guidelines)
- **Contents page**
- **Lists of tables and figures**
- **Literature review**
- **Methodology**
- **Results**
- **Discussion**
- **References**
- **Appendices:**
  - Any **forms or documents** you have referred to in the text, in order of appearance in the main dissertation. Your appendices should be labelled alphabetically according to APA guidelines, so the first appendix should be appendix A, then B, C, etc. Include the **participant information sheet, consent form, debrief**, and any **tests, measures** or **scales** used in the methodology.
  - **Library waiver-** signed (does not need to be referred to in the text)
  - **Your meeting logs-** if this is not available you need to include a document signed by you and your supervisor stating the approximate number of meetings and general support offered (as appendix, again not to be referred to in text)
  - **Proof of ethical approval-** a copy of your ethical approval certificate, and copies of email exchanges approving any changes that have been made.
  - **Raw data-** either transcripts of interviews (if conducted) or the SPSS output from your analysis (if quantitative). Discuss these requirements with your supervisor if you are unsure. Note that you may also be asked to produce the raw data file(s) at a later date, so keep these safe just in case!

Remember: All appendices need to be referred to in text except the library waiver and your meeting logs!

Finally please remember that the **word count is 7,000 to 10,000 words**. This excludes tittle, abstract, references and appendices. You are permitted 10%+/–. *Please note that word length will be checked and any dissertation exceeding this will be subject to a standard penalty of the deduction of one percentage point per 100 words (or part thereof) where the limit is exceeded.*

Communicating Research: Preparing Manuscripts, Posters and Talks

Privitera, G. J.

Communicating what was found in a research study is just as important as the finding itself. Albert Einstein said, "If you can't explain it simply, you don't understand it well enough." Being able to communicate what you found, then, is important inasmuch as it not only allows others to understand what you found but also makes clear to others that you understand the finding as well. In this way, your ability to effectively communicate in science can reflect your fundamental credibility as an author.

As a student, you can appreciate fully the value of communicating ideas. In the classroom, you often categorize professors as being good or bad teachers based on how well they could explain or make sense of the material being taught in class. Professors who made sense of difficult material in class often receive higher ratings than professors who are obviously knowledgeable but unable to effectively communicate that knowledge in the classroom. In a similar way, a scientist has the responsibility to make sense of the findings or ideas discovered in a research study. After all, it is of little value to be unable to communicate new knowledge to others. In fact, Einstein himself believed that "any fool can know. The point is to understand." Communicating research findings, then, can be as important as the discovery itself.

In this chapter, we will introduce the methods of communication in research: manuscripts, posters, and talks. Throughout this chapter, we focus largely on how to effectively communicate ideas using each method and we provide tips and strategies to help you in your own work. Following the guidelines described in this chapter can give you the tools you need to effectively appeal your ideas to a diverse audience and allow you to present yourself as an authoritative, credible, and engaging communicator.

15.1 Elements of Communication

Oral and written reports can exist for long periods of time and contribute to a large body of knowledge in the behavioral sciences. Scientific research is a collaborative effort in which groups of researchers from different universities and institutions across the globe converge to describe their research and interpretations on a topic. Common methods of communication for researchers include publishing their work in a peer-reviewed journal and participating in some of the many conferences held each year all over the world, in which researchers gather to report their most current findings in a poster or introduce their new ideas in a talk. When a manuscript is published in a peer-reviewed journal, it is integrated into the accepted scientific body of knowledge and made available for criticism and review by other scientists who accept or reject the ideas presented in that publication. Likewise, a poster or talk can open the lines of communication between scientists in a way that allows them to share ideas to facilitate a more grounded understanding of a topic in the behavioral sciences.

Three methods of communication are to publish a manuscript, present a poster, and prepare a talk.

Writing a manuscript for publication, presenting a poster, and preparing a talk are three key methods of communication among scientists. In this chapter, we introduce the American Psychological Association (APA, 2009) style for formatting and writing manuscripts, and we provide tips and strategies for presenting a poster and giving a talk. First, we introduce three basic elements of communication: the speaker (or author), the audience, and the message. Each element of communication is also summarized in Table 15.1 at the end of this section.

The Speaker or Author

As a speaker or author, you are responsible for mediating a communication. How you communicate will be important in how your message is received by an audience. For a manuscript, it is important to communicate using the following APA guidelines:

1. Use first person and third person appropriately. In APA style, use the first person to discuss research steps rather than anthropomorphizing the work. For example, a study cannot "manipulate" or "hypothesize"; you and your coauthors, however, can (e.g., "We manipulated the levels of the variable..." or "We hypothesized that changes would occur..."). Also use first-person singular (i.e., "I") if you are a sole author; use first-person plural (i.e., "we") when referring to work you completed with many authors. Use the third person, however, to foreground the research. For example, state, "The results indicate..." and *not* "We found evidence..." to report the findings of a study—the study, not the authors, elicits data. The most important suggestion is to be clear and avoid confusion in your writing. For example, "We are facing an obesity epidemic..." may leave the reader wondering whether *we* refers to the authors of the article, to community members, or to some other group. In these cases, *we* can still be an appropriate referent with a simple rewrite (e.g., "As Americans, *we* are facing

an obesity epidemic..."), or the third person can be used (e.g., "Americans are facing an obesity epidemic...").

2. Use past, present, and future tense appropriately. To describe previous research, use past tense. For example, state, "The data showed that..." or "Previous work demonstrated that..." to describe published or completed work. Also use past tense to describe your results for completed work, such as "Scores increased from Time 1 to Time 2" or "The data were significant." In the discussion, you can use present tense to describe current work, such as "To address these concerns, we are conducting several follow-up studies." Use future tense to describe events or work that will occur or be completed at a later time.

3. Use an impersonal writing style. A research manuscript is not a novel, so avoid the use of literary devices beyond what is necessary. For example, avoid using colloquial devices such as "over the top" (in place of "exaggerated") and avoid jargon such as "techy" (in place of "technologically savvy"). Also, use language appropriately. For example, to give a reason for an event or method use "because" and not "since" (e.g., "male participants were excluded *because*...") because "since" indicates the passage of time (e.g., "These studies have not been replicated *since* before 2000"). As another example, to describe something that does not refer to a location, use "in which" and not "where" (e.g., "participants completed a survey *in which* all items pertained to...") because "where" indicates a location (e.g., "Participants were situated at the back of a room, *where* a series of items were located").

4. Reduce biased language. The author can use unbiased language in two ways. First, follow APA guidelines for using unbiased language, as discussed in greater detail in Section 15.2, with examples given in Table 15.2. For example, people with a disorder should be characterized as a person and not by their disorder. To avoid bias, we state "Participants with depression" instead of "Depressed participants," for example. Second, do not use language in a manuscript that would be offensive to others, particularly our colleagues and fellow researchers. For example, to describe the limitations in another study, state, "Gender *was not included* as a factor" instead of "Previous researchers *completely ignored* gender as a factor in their study."

5. Give credit where appropriate. The APA provides specific guidelines for citing sources that are published in the *Publication Manual of the American Psychological Association* (APA, 2009). Anytime you cite work that is not your own, make sure you give proper credit to the author of that work using these APA guidelines. Further details for properly citing sources are given in Section 15.3 in this chapter and also in Appendix A.

6. The perspective of writing using APA style is that the author reports about findings in a research study; the author does not tell about his or her research. In other words, it is the research itself, and not the researcher, that is the focus of the

report. The goal of communication is to persuade others based upon the methods and findings in a research report, and not by catchy literary devices or the actions of the researcher. While this goal also applies to poster presentations and talks, we do make one exception: It is preferred that the speaker uses primarily first person in these forums because posters and talks are interactive. The speaker communicates in real time to other researchers, so using first person more often can be more natural in these settings. Otherwise, the remaining guidelines should be followed to present a poster or give a talk.

The Audience

The audience is any individual or group with whom you intend to communicate. Although scientific data may often be completed at a level that is difficult to understand, it is often the case that the audience is more diverse than many authors recognize. For any scientific work, the authors should consider the following audiences who are likely to read their report:

1. Scientists and professionals. Scientists are those who work in university or laboratory settings. Professionals are those who work in industry or hospitals. These groups are interested in the methods and procedures of your work, as well as your ideas and interpretations of the outcomes. Scientists and professionals are educated in your field or general discipline. They can also often be among the most critical audiences to evaluate the contributions of your research and ideas because they are often in the best position, in terms of funding and resources, to challenge your results and interpretations and to produce their own research to demonstrate the validity of their challenges. Because these groups tend to be the most critical of a research study, most authors tend to write or speak mostly to these groups.

2. College students. It is likely that more students read scientific reports and attend poster sessions and talks each year than those with terminal and professional degrees. Doctoral graduate students, for example, must complete a dissertation and spend many years and endless hours integrating a body of research to develop a research idea and conduct a study worthy of earning a doctoral degree. Undergraduate students often review articles in published works as part of class assignments or attend conferences to gain experience needed for acceptance to graduate programs. College students are likely to be your largest audience and yet they have less background or understanding of the topic being communicated than scientists and professionals. Providing sufficient background of the research topic and defining or operationalizing key factors in a research study can facilitate an understanding of your work among this group.

3. The general public (laypersons). Many persons in the general public can find and read your work. For example, when parents learn that a member of their family has a behavioral disorder, they can use problem-focused coping strategies to learn

more about what is known of a disorder and the potential treatment options for that disorder. In these cases, it is useful to make an effort to communicate data effectively such that this general nonscientific audience can also understand the gist or importance of the findings of a given report.

The audiences with which we share our ideas and works are often larger than we recognize. Consider also that there is a growing popularity in the publication of open-access articles, such as those in open-access peer-reviewed journals published by BioMed Central and Scientific Research Publishing. Open-access articles are peer-reviewed works that are freely available to scientists, professionals, students, and the general public. The direction of publication, then, is to expand the size of an audience by enhancing how accessible research is, which makes it more pertinent than ever for the author or speaker to effectively communicate to this broader audience.

The Message

The author or speaker communicates the message, which is any information regarding the design, analyses, interpretations, and new ideas contributed by a completed research project or literature review. The message is important inasmuch as an audience understands it. To effectively communicate a message, we should consider the following guidelines:

1. The message should be novel. A novel idea is one that is original or new. You must be able to explain and demonstrate in your work how your ideas add to or build upon the scientific literature. If you can demonstrate what we learn from your ideas, then your ideas are novel.

2. The message should be interesting. An interesting idea can potentially benefit society, test a prediction, or develop areas of research in which little is known. Peer-reviewed journals have a readership, and your idea must appeal to those who read that journal if you are to publish your ideas.

3. The message should be informative. An informative message is one that provides a thorough description of a work. For example, the literature should be fully reviewed, the details of research procedures should be fully described, and all data measured in a study should be fully reported. Hence, do not omit information that would be otherwise informative to an audience to determine the extent to which a work is novel and interesting.

For a speaker or author to effectively communicate a message to an audience, it is important to consider the three elements of communication described in this section. The implication of each element suggests that delivering an appropriate, novel, interesting, and informative message to a broad audience will significantly enhance the effectiveness of the communication of a work. Table 15.1 summarizes each element of communication described in this section.

| Table 15.1 | Three Elements of Communication |

Elements of Communication	General Characteristics
The speaker or author	Use appropriate verb tense. Use an impersonal writing style. Reduce biased language. Give credit where appropriate.
The audience	Scientists and professionals. College students. The general public (laypeople).
The message	The message should be novel. The message should be interesting. The message should be informative.

LEARNING CHECK 1 ✓

1. State three methods of communication.

2. State three elements in communication.

3. True or false: Delivering an appropriate, novel, interesting, and informative message to a broad audience will significantly enhance the effectiveness of the communication of a work.

Answers: 1. Publish a manuscript, present a poster, or prepare a talk; 2. The speaker or author, the audience, and the message; 3. True.

15.2 Writing a Manuscript: Writing Style and Language

The most critical method of communication is to publish a work in a peer-reviewed journal, which is any publication that is subjected to a peer review. A peer review is a procedure used by scientific journals in which a manuscript or work is sent to peers or experts in that area to review the work and determine its scientific value or worth regarding publication. Only upon acceptance from these peer reviewers will a work be published in a peer-reviewed journal. The peer review process is demanding because of the high rejection rates

Peer review is a procedure used by the editors of scientific journals in which a manuscript or work is sent to peers or experts in that area to review the work and determine its scientific value or worth regarding publication.

of works submitted to a journal for consideration for publication. Many of these journals reject from 75% to 85% or more of the manuscripts they receive each year. For this reason, publishing a work in a peer-reviewed journal is regarded as a high achievement in the scientific community.

> An APA-style manuscript is a document that is created using the writing style format detailed in the *Publication Manual of the American Psychological Association*, typically for the purposes of having the work considered for publication in a peer-reviewed journal.

To submit a work for consideration for publication in a peer-reviewed journal, we prepare a document called an APA-style manuscript. An APA-style manuscript is a document that is created using the formatting style detailed in the *Publication Manual of the American Psychological Association* (APA, 2009), abbreviated as the *Publication Manual*. APA style is required by over 1,000 research journals worldwide and across disciplines. The *Publication Manual* provides guidelines for writing an APA-style manuscript and should always be referred to when writing a manuscript using this writing style.

> Accuracy in a scientific report is important because it reflects the credibility of the author.

In this section, and in Sections 15.3 and 15.4, we will introduce the writing style described in the *Publication Manual*. This chapter is meant to be an overview of writing using APA style. For a more exhaustive description of this writing style, please refer to the *Publication Manual*. In this section, we introduce four general writing guidelines: Be accurate; be comprehensive, yet concise; be conservative; and be appropriate.

Be Accurate

When writing an APA-style manuscript, or any type of paper for that matter, the sources you cite, the interpretations you provide, the data you report, and the grammar and writing you present must be accurate. Accuracy in a manuscript is important because it reflects the credibility of the author. Writing a manuscript with even just one error can damage the credibility of the author and, depending on how serious the mistake, can lead the audience to question the accuracy of other aspects of the report, even when the other parts of the work are accurate. Keep in mind that to be able to persuade others of the value of a work, the researcher must have credibility with the audience. Losing credibility due to mistakes is often avoidable and is seen as the result of sloppy writing and poor revision. To avoid this problem, we can apply a common method: proofread a paper or manuscript, put it down for a day or two, proofread it again, then let a friend or colleague proofread it before making final changes. This method can be used to eliminate many errors that may have been otherwise overlooked or ignored.

Be Comprehensive, Yet Concise

Being comprehensive means that you include enough information in your report that the reader is able to critically evaluate its contribution to the scientific literature. For a primary research study, for example, this means that the author fully discloses the procedures used and clearly identifies the hypotheses tested and why it was important to test those hypotheses. Being concise means that the author fully discloses his or her study in as few words as possible. It means that the author only makes arguments that are needed to support his or her hypotheses, and the author describes only as many details about the procedures and data so as to allow another author to replicate his or her design. Being comprehensive, yet concise, is important because it makes the manuscript easier to follow—it provides a full report, while also focusing only on information needed to make arguments and report the procedures and data. The following are four common strategies used to be comprehensive, yet concise, using APA style:

- Abbreviate where appropriate. Any terms that can be abbreviated or have a common abbreviation should be abbreviated after their first use. For example, to describe participants who exhibit high dietary restraint, we spell out *high dietary restraint* on first use with an abbreviation given in parentheses, and all subsequent references to the term can be abbreviated as HDR. For example, on first use we state, "Only participants exhibiting high dietary restraint (HDR) were..." On subsequent uses we only use the abbreviation HDR. Other common abbreviations include seconds (s), grams (g), compare (cf.), and post meridiem (p.m.), which are used to make the writing more concise.

- Display data in a figure or table. A figure or table can be particularly helpful when large data sets are reported. For example, to describe participant characteristics, we can report them in the text or in a table. The more characteristics to report, the more concise (and clear) it will be to summarize these characteristics in a table and not in the text. Likewise, any data analyses that are relevant to the hypotheses being tested should be described in a table or figure. In the text, you would only refer the reader to that figure or table. For example, you can state, "The groups all showed a significant increase in responding, as shown in Figure 1." The data for this result would then be given in the figure and not in the text.

- Avoid using unnecessary words and avoid using the passive voice: Write efficiently. At a macro-level, read through your paper and if you can remove a word, phrase, or sentence without losing the meaning of your content, then delete it. At a micro-level, preferentially use an active voice within each sentence because the passive voice often tends to be unnecessary or too wordy. For example, to describe your results in the passive voice, you could write, "Significance *was shown* in the analysis." However, the active voice is less wordy; it is thus more concise. We could revise this sentence to state, "The analysis *showed* significance." Here, we reduce a six-word sentence to a four-word sentence.

- Keep the writing focused. In other words, introduce only those ideas and research needed to persuade the reader of the value of your work or research hypotheses. For example, you may hypothesize that integrating technology in the classroom will improve student grades. In your literature review, then, you should review what we know about classrooms that integrate technology, student learning outcomes related to the use of technology, and how that literature relates to the hypotheses you are testing. You should not introduce any ideas or research other than that directly related to your hypothesis. Likewise, you should only display data in a figure or table that are directly related to your hypothesis and otherwise briefly summarize data that are not directly related to your hypothesis. Focused writing makes it easier for the reader to evaluate the value of your work.

- Do not repeat information. When you read over your own work, ask yourself: Does this sentence add information? If not, then delete it. When you introduce more than one study in a single report, ask yourself: Are the procedures in this study different from those I already introduced? If not, then do not introduce the procedures again; instead, refer the reader to where the procedures were originally introduced. For example, suppose you conduct two experiments using the same research design. In Experiment 1, introduce the full research design; for the second experiment, state, "same as those described for Experiment 1" for all procedures that repeat those already introduced. We avoid repetition in writing to make the writing style more concise. Being comprehensive, yet concise, is important because the space or the number of pages available in printed peer-reviewed journals is limited. To be published in peer-reviewed journals, then, many journal editors require that a manuscript fully describe a study that was conducted while also taking up as few printed pages as possible.

> Clearly state all essential information in as few words as possible.

Be Conservative

As part of any scientific writing style, it is important to be conservative in your claims and interpretations. In other words, do not generalize beyond the data or overstate your conclusions. For example, suppose we observe that women were significantly more willing to offer to help a bystander than men. An appropriately conservative conclusion is that women were more helpful in the experimental situation in our study. That is all we observed: helping behavior. We should not generalize beyond these specific observations. In other words, a statement like "Women were nicer than men" is inappropriate. We did not measure *niceness*; we measured *helping*. We can speculate about whether our observations indicate that women are nicer than men, but we must make it clear that this is just a speculation and that more research is required. As a general rule, do not make claims about anything that you did not directly measure or observe, or that others have not directly measured or observed. Be cautious in your writing. The strengths of your study will be in what you observed, so it is your observations, and not your speculations, that should be the focus of your interpretations in a manuscript.

> Do not generalize your claims or interpretations beyond the data; do not overstate your conclusions.

Be Appropriate

The *Publication Manual* provides detailed guidelines for using appropriate and unbiased language. Some of the guidelines in the *Publication Manual* are given in Table 15.2. The importance of using appropriate and unbiased language is to ensure that you do not offend those who read your work or those who are the subject of your work. For example, in the sixth row of Table 15.2, we find that it is biased to refer to individuals or groups by their disorder. Hence, it is biased to write "A sample of autistic patients were studied" because we are identifying the group by its disorder. Instead, we should write "A sample of patients with autism were studied." It may seem like a subtle change, but in the first sentence, we identified the group as being defined by its disorder, which could be viewed as offensive. In the revised sentence, we identified autism as one characteristic of this group, which is more appropriate and less biased.

Table 15.2   Examples for Using Unbiased Language

Do Not Use:	Instead Use:
"homosexuals"	"gay men and lesbians"
"sexual preference"	"sexual orientation"
"men" (referring to all adults)	"men and women"
"black" or "white" (referring to social groups)	"Black" or "White" (capitalized)
ethnic labels (e.g., "Oriental")	geographical labels (e.g., "Asian" or "Asian American")
"victims" or "disordered" (to characterize people)	"people with _____" (e.g., "People with autism")
"case"	"patient"
"sex" (referring to a culture or social role)	"gender"
"gender" (referring to biology)	"sex"
"subjects" (referring to humans)	"participants"
"participants" (referring to animals)	"subjects"

Adapted from the Publication Manual (APA, 2009).

LEARNING CHECK 2 ✓

1. What is a peer review?

2. Why is it important to be accurate?

3. State four common strategies used to be comprehensive yet concise using APA style.

4. A researcher measured grades on an exam in two classes and concluded that students in Class 2 scored higher and so must have enjoyed the class more. Is this a conservative conclusion? Explain.

5. Why is it important to use appropriate and unbiased language?

15.3 Elements of an APA-Style Manuscript

Using APA style is as much an editorial style as it is a writing style. The elements of an APA-style manuscript are structured so that the manuscript can be readily typeset and converted to a published document. Having a formatting style that is readily converted to a published document is convenient for editors who, upon acceptance following a peer review, will publish the manuscript in their journal. An APA-style manuscript is organized into the following major sections, each of which is described in this section:

- Title page. The title page is always the first page and includes a running head, the title, a list of the author or authors, affiliations, and an author note with the contact information of the primary (contact) author.

- Abstract. The abstract is always the second page and provides a brief written summary of the purpose, methods, and results of a work or published document in 150 to 250 words.

- Main body. The main body begins on page 3 of a manuscript. The main body is divided into subsections and most often includes the following main subheadings: (1) an introduction section that includes a literature review and identification of research hypotheses; (2) a method section that describes the participants, surveys and materials, procedures, and analyses; (3) a results section that fully discloses the data measured and statistical outcomes observed; and (4) a discussion section that provides an evaluation of the design, the data, and the hypotheses.

- References. The references page always follows the main body on a new page. All sources cited in the manuscript are listed in alphabetical order in APA format in this section.

- Footnotes (if any). Footnotes are used to provide additional content (such as clarification about a procedure or outcome) or acknowledge copyright permissions. Many manuscripts are written without needing a footnotes section; however, if this section is included in the manuscript, then it should immediately follow the references section.

- Tables (if any). Tables can be included, often to summarize participant data or data analyses. Each table is given on a separate page after the references section (or after the footnotes section if included). Table captions are included above or below each table on each page.

- Figures (if any). Figures can be included, often to summarize data analyses or illustrate a research procedure. Each figure is given on a separate page following the tables. Figure captions are included above or below each figure on each page.

- Appendices (if any). In some cases there may be supplemental materials, such as surveys, illustrations, or instructions for using complex equipment. Many manuscripts are written without needing an appendix; however, if this section is included, then it should be at the end of the manuscript.

Next we will review the sections that are most often included in a manuscript: the title page, abstract, main body (introduction, methods and results, and discussion), and references. As an illustration for each section of an APA manuscript, we will use a manuscript that was completed by an undergraduate student at St. Bonaventure University under the advisement of the first author. This manuscript has since been accepted for publication in a peer-reviewed journal (Privitera & Creary, 2013), and a follow-up to this study was subsequently published (Privitera & Zuraikat, 2014). For more detailed APA guidelines including creating margins, page numbers, and running heads, refer to Appendix A, which gives an APA writing guide (A.1), an APA guide to grammar, punctuation, and spelling (A.2), and a full sample APA-style manuscript from a study that was published in a peer-reviewed scientific journal (A.3).

Title Page

The title page allows an editor to identify the individuals and affiliations of those who have significantly contributed to the work being described in the manuscript. This page is often the only page in which authors identify themselves, which can allow editors at many journals to send out a manuscript for an anonymous peer review by omitting the title page before sending the rest of the manuscript to reviewers. All required parts of a title page are illustrated in Figure 15.1.

The title page includes a running head in all capital letters that is a maximum of 50 characters, and the first page number is aligned to the right. All subsequent pages will also have a running head, but the words "Running Head" will be omitted. In addition to a running head, we include the title, author or authors, affiliations, and author note, which are centered on the title page. The title should be no more than 12 words, although it can exceed this total if needed to convey important information to the potential reader. The author note should include the contact information for only one author who is deemed the contact author, or the author with whom the editor (and readers of the research, if it is published) will correspond regarding the manuscript.

> The title page is the first page of a manuscript and includes the title, authors, affiliations, and author note.

Abstract

The abstract, shown in Figure 15.2, is the second page and provides a brief written summary of the purpose, methods, and results of a work or published document in 150 to 250 words. The words "Running Head" are removed from the header on this page and all other pages of the manuscript. The structure of an abstract can differ depending on the type of study being described. For APA manuscripts that describe primary research (i.e., the conduct of an experiment or research study), the following components should be described in an abstract:

- An opening sentence of the hypothesis or research problem being tested.
- A description of participants (e.g., number, sex, or age) if pertinent to outcomes. For animal research, the genus and species can be given.

Figure 15.1 APA-Style Title Page

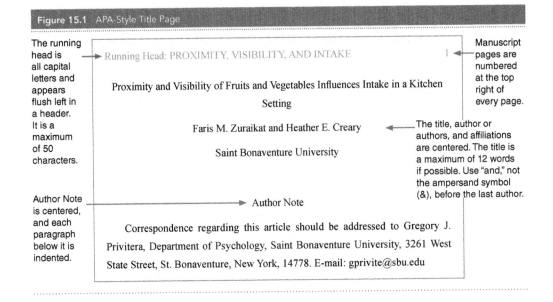

The running head is all capital letters and appears flush left in a header. It is a maximum of 50 characters.

Running Head: PROXIMITY, VISIBILITY, AND INTAKE   1

Proximity and Visibility of Fruits and Vegetables Influences Intake in a Kitchen Setting

Faris M. Zuraikat and Heather E. Creary

Saint Bonaventure University

Manuscript pages are numbered at the top right of every page.

The title, author or authors, and affiliations are centered. The title is a maximum of 12 words if possible. Use "and," not the ampersand symbol (&), before the last author.

Author Note is centered, and each paragraph below it is indented.

Author Note

Correspondence regarding this article should be addressed to Gregory J. Privitera, Department of Psychology, Saint Bonaventure University, 3261 West State Street, St. Bonaventure, New York, 14778. E-mail: gprivite@sbu.edu

- The essential structure or procedures of the research design used.

- The basic findings, which can include *p* values, confidence intervals, or effect sizes.

- A one- or two-sentence conclusion indicating the implications or applications of the research outcomes.

An abstract is a brief summary of the purpose, methods, and results of a work in 150 to 250 words.

An abstract can be the most important paragraph in your manuscript because many potential readers, if not interested in your research after reading the abstract, will not be likely to read on. For this reason, make sure you use keywords in your abstract that will appeal to potential readers and words you anticipate that potential readers would use as keywords in online searches. Following these suggestions can help get your work noticed by potential readers.

Introduction

The introduction begins on page 3 with the title restated on the first line. On the second line, indent the first paragraph and begin the introduction. An introduction must clearly communicate what makes your ideas novel and interesting in about two to three pages. Your ideas should be novel inasmuch as they build on previous research. Your ideas should be interesting inasmuch as they appeal to the readership of the journal to which you submit your work. The structure of an introduction should use the following organization:

Figure 15.2 An APA-Style Abstract

"Abstract" is centered on the top line. The paragraph below it is not indented.

The body of the abstract describes the hypotheses, participants, research design, basic findings, and implications in 150 to 250 words.

Italicize and center a list of 4 to 5 keywords.

PROXIMITY, VISIBILITY, AND INTAKE   2

Abstract

The hypothesis that participants will eat more fruits (apples) and vegetables (carrots) if they are made more proximate and visible was tested using a 2 × 2 between-subjects design. Proximity was manipulated by placing fruits and vegetables in a bowl at a table where participants sat (near) or 2 m from the table (far). Visibility was manipulated by placing fruits and vegetables in an opaque bowl that was covered (not visible) or in a clear bowl that was open (visible). The results showed that placing apples and carrots in closer proximity to participants increased intake of these healthy foods. Making these foods more visible increased intake of apples, but not carrots, possibly because fruits taste sweet and so may be more visually appealing. Regardless, these data are the first to demonstrate experimentally that the proximity and visibility of healthy foods can influence intake of these foods.

Keywords: proximity, visibility, fruits, vegetables, for convenience

- Introduce the problem and explain why it is important to conduct new research to address the problem. For example:

  o "The impact of environmental factors on food intake and consumption volume is of particular interest to researchers because such factors can lead to overeating and potential risks of obesity." In this first sentence of the introduction illustrated in Figure 15.3, we identified the problem (the impact of environmental factors on food intake) and why it is important to conduct research to address this problem (because environmental factors can lead to overeating and potential risks of obesity).

- Integrate previous research that is relevant to the research you are conducting to address the problem. You must thoroughly review the literature and include any and all research that could impact the validity of your claims and the value of your research. Providing appropriate credit is the responsibility of each author and contributes to the growth of scientific understanding across studies and disciplines. Also keep in mind the following suggestions:

Figure 15.3   Excerpt From an APA-Style Introduction

The introduction begins on page 3 with the running head.

The title is centered on line 1.

The introduction begins on line 2 and is indented.

> PROXIMITY, VISIBILITY, AND INTAKE   3
>
> Proximity and Visibility of Fruits and Vegetables Influences Intake in a Kitchen Setting
>
> The impact of environmental factors on food intake and consumption volume
> is of particular interest to researchers because such factors can lead to overeating
> and potential risks of obesity (Swinburn, Sacks, McPherson, Finegood, Moodie, &
> Gortmaker, 2011). Environmental factors that influence consumption volume include
> the portion sizes of foods in a meal (Wansink & Kim, 2005; Krim, Roe, & Rolls, 2004),
> mere exposure to foods (Pliner, 1982; Birch & Marlin, 1982), sensory characteristics
> of foods (Bell, Roe & Rolls, 2003; Kral, 2006), reward and punishment (Hendy, 1999;
> Batsell & Brown, 2002), cognition (Capaldi, Owens, & Privitera, 2006), social context
> (Birch, Zimmerman, & Hind, 1980), time of day (Rozin & Tuorila, 1993), and other
> factors related to family, society, culture, and media influences (see Privitera, 2008). Two

Use an ampersand (&) to give a reference in parentheses; use the word "and" when a reference is given in the text.

> factors that can cova
> food from an individ
> example, foods serv
> is more proximate an
> In an early inve
> intake, Terry and Be
> obese families, but in
> Herman Hackett, an
> and consumed less v
> participants being

> PROXIMITY, VISIBILITY, AND INTAKE   5
>
> The results in these previous studies raise an important question
> for dieters and health professionals alike: Does the proximity and visibility
> of fruits and vegetables also influence intake of healthier foods? Fruits and
> vegetables do not require preparation to eat and are often not wrapped,
> meaning that we should find that proximate and visible fruits and vegetables
> are consumed more. An early study using survey data suggests that the more
> proximate and visible parents make fruits and vegetables, the more elementary
> school children will eat them (Hearn, Baranowski, Baranowski, Doyle, Smith,
> Lin, & Resnicow, 1998). To date, these findings have not been supported using
> an experimental research design, and of the studies using experimental designs
> to test food. In the present study, we adapted the experimental design used
> by Wansink et al. (2006) to determine whether the proximity and visibility
> of apples (fruit) and carrots (vegetable) in a kitchen setting influences intake
> of these healthier foods using a between-subjects design. A between-subjects
> design was used to minimize demand characteristics caused by changing the
> location of the experimental foods.

The beginning of the introduction on page 3 and the last paragraph of the introduction on page 5 are shown in the figure.

- o Do not review the history of your topic; review only those articles that directly impact your claims and research. Do not describe details of those works that are not pertinent to your work.
- o Cite all sources appropriately. In the text, use "and" to separate the last author; in parentheses, use the ampersand symbol (&).
- o Although you must be concise in your writing, make sure that your writing can be clearly understood by the audience to which you are writing.

- State the hypotheses being tested and the research design being used to address the problem. State how you plan to address the problem in a way that will build upon (not repeat) the literature. For example:

  - o "To date... of the studies using experimental designs to test proximity and visibility, all have used junk food or candies as the test food. In the present study, we adapted the experimental design... to determine whether the proximity and visibility of apples (fruit) and carrots (vegetable) in a kitchen setting influences intake of these healthier foods using a between-subjects design." In this sentence, in the last paragraph of the introduction for the manuscript illustrated in Figure 15.3, we identified the hypothesis tested (proximity and visibility of fruits and vegetables influence intake) and the research design used (between-subjects design). We also identified how we will build upon the literature (by using fruits and vegetables, and not junk foods, as test foods). Notice that by including information about our hypothesis, the rationale for the hypothesis being tested is also implied (to advance our understanding for how visibility and proximity influence intake of fruits and vegetables). If the rationale for a hypothesis is not clearly implied, you should state it directly.

> In an introduction, state a problem, review pertinent literature, and state why the problem is important, and how it will be addressed.

Method and Results

The "Method" section immediately follows the introduction. As shown in Figure 15.4, we bold and center "Method" on the line below the last line of the introduction. On the next line we indent and begin the "Method" section. The "Method" section is divided with many subheadings. The major subheadings—"Participants," "Procedures," "Data Analyses," and "Results"—are described here and illustrated in Figure 15.4.

- The "Participants" subheading is flush left and bold, as shown in Figure 15.4. The "Participants" section should include full details of the participants, such as age, weight, and height. The specific characteristics of participants can be listed in a table or in the text. Also, state how participants in the sample compare to the target population of interest, which sampling method was used to select the participants, and how the total number of participants was determined.

- The "Procedures" subheading follows the "Participants" section and is flush left and bold, as shown in Figure 15.4. The "Procedures" section must describe how participants were treated with enough information so as to allow the reader to fully replicate the procedures. When portions of the procedures make the writing more concise and easier to follow if presented apart from the "Procedures"

Figure 15.4   Excerpts From APA-Style "Method" and "Results" Sections

influences intake of these healthier foods using a between-subjects design. A
between-subjects design was used to minimize demand characteristics caused
by changing the location of the experimental foods.

Center "Method" in bold on the line below the last line of the introduction (not on a separate page).

Method

The experiment was separated into two variations. In Variation 1,
the location of a bowl of apples (fruit) was manipulated using one sample.
In Variation 2, the location of a bowl of carrots (vegetable) was manipulated
using a different sample. In all, a total of 96 participants ($n = 48$ per
variation) were observed in this study. Otherwise, all procedures described
here were identical in each variation.

Place "Participants," flush left and in bold, on the line below the last line of the "Method" section.

Participants

A total of 96 participants (24 men, 72 women) were recruited

Include a "Procedures" section, flush left and in bold, on the line below the "Participants" section. If portions can be more clearly presented under their own heading—e.g., a description of surveys or, in this case, a setting and foods—then do so before the "Procedures" section as shown.

thr
ate within two hours of the study were excluded from data analyses. The
par university's Institutional Review Board approved the procedures for this study.
= 2

Va

Setting and Stimuli

Kitchen setting. All experimental foods were consumed in a kitchen

se

Procedures

pa

All procedures were conducted in a laboratory setting between 2:00

In

p.r

Add "Data Analyses," flush left and in bold. This section is optional in some journals but required by other journals.

"Results" is centered in bold. All statistical outcomes are reported in this section.

Data Analyses

wa ex
Th ca
sin the
re bo
we
the

In each variation, a 2×2 between-subjects analysis of variance
(ANOVA) was computed with proximity (near, far) and visibility (yes, no) as
between-subject factors. Gender and BMI were added as factors to determine
whether these factors influenced intakes. A Tukey's HSD was used as the post
hoc test where appropriate. All tests were conducted at a .05 level of significance.

Results

in
Pr
the
the
bo
gr

Variation 1 (apples). A Proximity × Visibility interaction was significant,
$F(3, 44) = 4.75, p < .04$ ($R^2 = .10$). As shown in Figure 1, participants consumed
the most apples when they were both convenient and visible (6.0 vs. 1.6, Tukey's
HSD, $p < .001$). A main effect of proximity, $F(1, 44) = 25.46, p < .001$ ($R^2 = .37$),
and a main effect of visibility, was significant, and showed that more apples were
consumed when they were placed in closer proximity to the participant.

subheading, this is acceptable. If portions of the "Procedures" section are introduced separately, then give that portion its own subheading before the "Procedures" section, as shown in Figure 15.4 for describing a unique kitchen setting and food stimuli.

The "Method" section is divided into four main subheadings: "Participants," "Procedures" (can be further divided into subheadings), "Data Analyses" (may be optional), and "Results."

- The "Data Analyses" subheading follows the "Procedures" section and is flush left and bold, as shown in Figure 15.4. This section is not required using APA style; however, it is required by many journals that use APA-style formatting. If this section is required, then indicate the statistical tests and criterion used for each analysis that will be reported in the "Results" section that follows.

- The "Results" subheading follows the "Procedures" section and is centered and bold, as shown in Figure 15.4. Fully report all statistical outcomes in this section; however, make sure you place particular emphasis on the results that specifically address the research hypothesis being tested. Report the group means and standard deviations of measured outcomes and the test statistic, significance, effect size, and confidence intervals for statistical outcomes using APA style. Be thorough in the exposition of data, yet provide only enough detail in this section to help the reader understand how the outcomes reported relate to the hypotheses that were tested. Note that sample APA-style write-ups for statistical results have been provided throughout this book.

Discussion

The "Discussion" heading is centered and bolded on the line below the last line of the "Results" section, as shown in Figure 15.5. On the next line, indent the first paragraph and begin the discussion. In the discussion, you will evaluate and interpret the outcomes in your study. Do not use the discussion to restate points that were already made in the manuscript; instead, use the discussion to build upon or facilitate a stronger interpretation and understanding of the problem that was studied. The structure of a discussion should use the following organization:

- Clearly state whether the findings lend support or nonsupport for the hypothesis that was tested. Briefly explain where in the data the support or nonsupport was observed. For example:
  - In the last sentence of the first paragraph of the discussion in Figure 15.5, the authors state a clear message of support and nonsupport for their research hypothesis: "For vegetables, then, the hypothesis tested here was only partly supported in that no effect of visibility was observed."

- Give context for how your findings fit with previously published studies (studies that were likely first described in the introduction). For example:
  - In the second paragraph of the discussion in Figure 15.5, the authors give the following explanation for how their results could fit with previously published studies: "One likely explanation... is that apples may be more visually appealing than carrots because sweet-tasting foods are more visually appealing than bitter-tasting foods, and there is evidence to support such an explanation."

Figure 15.5 Excerpts From an APA-Style "Discussion" Section

that participants ate (1.4 vs. 0.3). Intakes did not significantly differ by gender or BMI across groups ($p > .65$ for all tests).

Center "Discussion" in bold on the line below the last line of the "Results" section.

Discussion

The hypothesis that making fruits and vegetables more proximate and visible will increase intake of these foods was tested. For fruits, participants consumed more apples when they were made more proximate and visible, i.e., in an open clear bowl within arms reach of the participant. For vegetables, however, participants consumed more carrots only when they were made, pre proximate (within arms reach of the participant). For vegetables, then, the hypothesis tested here was only partly supported in that no effect of visibility was observed.

Include a statement of support and nonsupport of the hypothesis tested.

PROXIMITY, VISIBILITY, AND INTAKE   10

Describe how findings relate to previously published studies.

One likely explanation for the different results observed for apples and carrots is that apples may be more visually appealing than carrots because sweet-tasting foods are more visually appealing than bitter-tasting foods, and there is evidence to support such an explanation (see Capaldi & Privitera, 2008; Privitera, 2008). Also, participants knew the fruits or vegetables were fresh and good to eat because foods were served from fresh sealed packages in front of each participant.

Identify potential limitations.

Whether the results would be different if fruits and vegetables were placed in a bowl before participants entered the room, or if the setting was different, such as in a workplace or office setting, cannot be determined here.

Summarize and provide commentary on the importance of the research findings.

At present, these results extend survey findings with parents and children (Hearn et al., 1998) and experimental findings with adults (Painter et al., 2002; Wansink et al., 2006) by showing the first data to demonstrate experimentally that the proximity and visibility of fruits (apples) and vegetables (carrots) in a kitchen setting influences intake of these healthier foods. In all, these results show that overeating may be food for health, so long as the environment consists of fruits and vegetables in the most proximate and visible locations.

- Identify potential limitations of your research and methods, imprecision of measures that may have biased the pattern of results observed, and any potential threats to internal or external validity. It is important to be conservative; identify what could be improved to make the reader more confident in the findings you observed. For example:

  o In the second paragraph of the discussion in Figure 15.5, the authors also identify a potential limitation for their study: "Whether the results would be different if fruits and vegetables were placed in a bowl before participants entered the room, or if the setting was different, such as in a workplace or office setting, cannot be determined here."

- Provide a brief summary or commentary on the importance of your findings, as shown in the last paragraph of the discussion in Figure 15.5. In a sentence or two, state how your findings are novel (build upon what is known in the literature) and interesting (to the readership of the journal to which you are submitting your work). You can also speculate as to what new directions of research could be pursued, given the results you observed, and the implications for such research.

References

The "References" heading begins on a separate page after the "Discussion" section. The word "References" is centered and bolded at the top of the page, and each source that was cited in the manuscript is listed in alphabetical order in this section, as shown in Figure 15.6. The appropriate citation for almost any type of source is provided in the *Publication Manual*. The most common sources cited are journal articles, books, and book chapters. We will describe the appropriate citation for each type of source in this section. For any other type of source, refer to the *Publication Manual*.

> In a "Discussion" section evaluate and interpret how the outcomes in a study relate to the problem or hypothesis that was tested.

To cite a journal article, list the author or authors, year of publication in parentheses, title of the article, name of the journal in italics, volume number in italics, issue number in parentheses (only if the journal is paginated by issue, not by volume), pages in the article, and digital object identifier (doi)—in that order. If a doi or an issue number is not available for an in-print article, then each can be omitted. The following citation is an example of a journal article reference (note that each reference in Figure 15.6 is for a journal article):

Privitera, G. J., & Dickinson, E. K. (2015). Control your cravings: Self-control varies by eating attitudes, sex, and food type among Division I collegiate athletes. *Psychology of Sport and Exercise, 19,* 18–22. doi:10.1016/j.psychsport.2015.02.004

To cite an entire book, list the author or authors, year of publication, title of the book with edition number in parentheses (if applicable), city and state of publication, and name of the publisher. For example, the following is an APA reference for the most recent

Figure 15.6 APA-Style "References" Section

Center "References" on the top line of a separate page.

Each reference is listed in alphabetical order, and the format for each reference is a hanging indent.

Always use the ampersand (&) symbol for listing the last author of a multiple-author reference.

Use the *Publication Manual* to find the correct citation for any type of reference. Note that all references shown here are for journal articles.

PROXIMITY, VISIBILITY, AND INTAKE   11

References

Baumgartner, E., & Laghi, F. (2012). Affective responses to movie posters: Differences between adolescents and young adults. *International Journal of Psychology, 47,* 154–160. doi:10.1080/00207594.2011.597398

Dalton, M., Blundell, J., & Finlayson, G. (2010). Effect of BMI and binge eating on food reward and energy intake: Further evidence for a binge eating subtype of obesity. *Obesity Facts, 6,* 348–359. doi:10.1159/000354599

Drewnowski, A. (2004). Obesity and the food environment: Dietary energy density and diet costs. *American Journal of Preventative Medicine, 27,* 154–162. doi:10.1016/j.amepre.2004.06.011

Epstein, L. H., Leddy, J. J., Temple, J. L., & Faith, M. S. (2007). Food reinforcement and eating: A multilevel analysis. *Psychological Bulletin, 133,* 884–906. doi:10.1037/0033-2909.133.5.884

---

edition of the *Publication Manual*; the second reference is for a book publication that is not published in editions:

American Psychological Association. (2009). *Publication manual of the American Psychological Association* (6th ed.). Washington, DC: Author.

Brookes, G., Pooley, J. A., & Earnest, J. (2015). *Terrorism, trauma and psychology: A multilevel victim perspective of the Bali bombings.* New York, NY: Routledge/Taylor & Francis Group.

The "References" section is an alphabetical list of all sources cited in a manuscript.

Many books are edited and not authored, meaning different authors contribute a chapter to a book that is then edited or assembled by a few of those contributors. For an edited book, then, it is very likely that a specific chapter in that book, and not the entire book, was the source you used. To cite a book chapter, list the author or authors of the book chapter, year of publication in parentheses, name of chapter, name of the editor or editors of the book with "Eds." given in parentheses after all names are listed, title of the book in italics, page numbers of the book chapter in parentheses, city and state of publication, and name of the publisher. If the book chapter is available electronically, then you can include the doi or uniform resource locator (URL). As an example, the following is a book chapter reference with a chapter contributed by two authors in a book with four editors:

> Fanselow, M. S., & Sterlace, S. R. (2014). Pavlovian fear conditioning: Function, cause, and treatment. In F. K. McSweeney, E. S. Murphy, F. K. McSweeney, E. S. Murphy (Eds.), *The Wiley Blackwell handbook of operant and classical conditioning* (pp. 117–141). Hoboken, NJ: Wiley-Blackwell. doi:10.1002/9781118468135.ch6

LEARNING CHECK 3 ✓

1. What is the maximum number of characters for a running head? What is the maximum number of words for a title?

2. What is the word limit for an abstract?

3. What are the four main sections of the main body of an APA-style manuscript?

4. In what order and with what type of formatting are references listed in a references section?

Answers: 1. The maximum is 50 characters for a running head, and 12 words for a title; 2. Between 150 and 250 words; 3. The introduction, methods, results, and discussion sections; 4. References are listed in alphabetical order using a hanging indent format.

15.4 Literature Reviews

An APA-style manuscript is typically written to report the findings of primary research, which is research conducted by the authors of a manuscript. However, it is also common to report on a review of literature in the form of a synthesis of previous articles or as a meta-analysis (Galvan, 2006). These types of reports, called literature review articles, are often submitted for publication in peer-reviewed journals as well. Because a literature review article follows a different organization from reports of primary research, we will introduce the unique organization of a literature review article in this section.

A literature review article is a written comprehensive report of findings from previously published works about a problem in the form of a synthesis of previous articles or as a meta-analysis.

A literature review article is a written comprehensive report of findings from previously published works in a specified area of research in the form of a synthesis of previous articles or as a meta-analysis. A literature review article can be chosen by research area (e.g., the motivational salience of primary rewards) or by a specific theme in an area of research (e.g., the use of a conditioned place preference design to study the motivational salience of primary rewards). The goal of a literature review article is to organize, integrate, and evaluate published works about a problem and to consider progress made toward clarifying that problem.

To write a literature review article, we include a title page, an abstract, a literature review (main body), and references. If footnotes, tables, figures, or appendices are included, then we can place them at the end of the manuscript following the references section using the same order introduced in Section 15.3. Two sections in a literature review article that differ from a manuscript or report of primary research are the abstract and the main body. In the abstract, identify the problem and give a synopsis of the evaluations made in the literature review using the same formatting and word count limits identified in Section 15.3. To write the main body, use the following organization:

- Identify the problem and how it will be evaluated. Identify the topic, keywords used to search for articles in that topic, and what search engines you used to find articles. Identify anything in your method of selecting articles that could bias the evaluations made in the literature review.

- Integrate the literature to identify the state of the research. In other words, identify what is known and what is not known. Be clear on how far we have advanced on an understanding of the problem being reviewed.

- Identify how findings and interpretations in the published literature are related or consistent, or are inconsistent, contradictory, or flawed. How confident can we be in what is known? For a meta-analysis, report effect sizes for the findings of many studies. Be critical of the samples used, the research designs implemented, and the data and interpretations made to address the problem.

- Consider the progress made in an area of research and potential next steps toward clarifying the problem. Identify what is not known and possible methods or advancements in technology that could be used to clarify the problem further.

The main body or literature review is the primary section of a literature review article. The entire review of the literature is contained in this one section. The main body or literature portion of the manuscript can have any headings and subheadings to organize the ideas and evaluations presented in the review. Major headings should be bold and flush left, with the text for that section beginning on the line below the major heading. In all, we can use the analogy of a puzzle to describe a literature review: It is an attempt to fit many puzzle pieces together, with the many articles published in a given area of research being the puzzle pieces in this analogy.

15.5 Reporting Observations in Qualitative Research

In Chapter 7 we introduced the qualitative research design as a method used to make nonnumeric observations, from which conclusions are drawn without the use of statistical analysis. The implication of not using statistical analysis is that the "Results" section in an APA-style manuscript is replaced with an "Analysis" section. A "Results" section in a quantitative study reports the statistical outcomes of the measured data; an "Analysis" section in a qualitative study provides a series of interpretations and contributes a new perspective or generates the possibility that many different perspectives can explain the observations made. For a qualitative analysis, then, the "Analysis" section is written as a narrative, and not as a report of statistical outcomes.

The "Results" section in an APA-style manuscript is replaced with an "Analysis" section for qualitative research designs.

Qualitative research is typically not directed by a hypothesis. In other words, researchers do not state a hypothesis and then limit their observations to measure only phenomena that are related to that hypothesis. Instead, qualitative researchers often use interviews, participant observation techniques, and field notes and allow participants to ask their own questions during the time that participants are observed. To analyze observations that are descriptive (i.e., written in words) and often guided by the questions that participants ask, researchers evaluate the *trustworthiness* of their observations, as introduced in Chapter 7 (see Table 7.2). Although this is certainly not an exhaustive list of differences, the following are two key differences in writing an APA-style manuscript for qualitative versus quantitative research:

- The introduction and the "Method" section in a qualitative report argue ways of examining a problem in a way that often leaves open many alternatives that were anticipated or not anticipated by the authors. This is unlike quantitative research, in which the introduction narrows in on one or more stated hypotheses upon which the "Method" section outlines what will be observed to test those hypotheses.

- In a qualitative report, a narrative is constructed in an "Analysis" section to describe what was observed. A "Discussion" section, then, evaluates possible explanations for those observations with little effort to generalize beyond the specific observations made. This is unlike quantitative research in which statistical outcomes are reported in a "Results" section. A "Discussion" section then focuses on whether the data showed support or nonsupport for the hypotheses tested.

For most qualitative research, the goal is to describe the experiences of an individual or a small group. The structure of the manuscript, then, takes the form of a narrative that leaves open many possible explanations and evaluates the extent to which those observations are trustworthy.

15.6 Ethics in Focus: Credit and Authorship

Authorship of a peer-reviewed work is a great achievement. In psychology, we expect the order of authorship to reflect the relative contributions of those listed as authors. The first author of a manuscript is the individual who contributed the most, with each subsequent author making relatively fewer contributions. Authors listed on the title page of a manuscript should be listed in order of their "relative scientific or professional contributions" (APA, 2010, p. 11) to the work being submitted to an editor or reviewer, and not based on their status or institutional position.

The challenges of authorship are in defining what constitutes "relative scientific or professional contributions." Is it the person who conducted the research, wrote the manuscript, developed the research hypothesis, or created the research design? Is it about the relative value of the ideas shared to contribute to the work, or is it in the time spent to complete the work? There is no one answer that can resolve what constitutes more or less "relative scientific or professional contributions." The APA suggests that to resolve any concerns regarding authorship, all potential authors should talk about publication credit as early as possible. Agreeing on the order of authorship prior to completing the work can facilitate less disagreement regarding the order of authorship later in the publication process.

LEARNING CHECK 4 ✓

1. What is the goal of a literature review?

2. What is reported in an "Analysis" section for a qualitative research study?

3. According to the APA, authors listed on the title page of a manuscript should be listed in order of their_____.

Answers: 1. The goal of a literature review is to organize, integrate, and evaluate published works about a problem and to consider progress made toward clarifying that problem; 2. An "Analysis" section in a qualitative study provides, in narrative form, a series of interpretations and contributes a new perspective or generates the possibility that many different perspectives can explain the observations made; 3. relative scientific or professional contributions.

15.7 Presenting a Poster

Aside from writing a manuscript, researchers and professionals often communicate by presenting a poster, which is a concise description of a research study in a display of text boxes, figures, and tables shown on a single large page. A poster is an eye-catching and engaging display that is typically presented during a poster session at a professional conference, such as those held annually by the APA,

A poster is a concise description of a research study in the form of a display of text boxes, figures, and tables on a single large page.

A poster session is a 1- to 4-hour time slot during which many authors stand near their poster ready and open to answer questions or talk about their work with interested attendees.

or at smaller venues. A poster session is a 1- to 4-hour time slot during which many authors stand near their poster ready and open to answer questions or talk about their work with interested attendees. To present a poster, you must submit an abstract of your work before the submission deadline of a conference. Upon acceptance of the abstract, you will receive a poster session time to present your poster.

Poster sessions can be exciting because researchers often present their most current work—so current that it has yet to be published in a peer-reviewed journal. For this reason, poster sessions can often give researchers a preview of the type of research that could be published in the coming year and generate many new ideas and directions for advancing research. Although thousands of poster sessions are held each year, the APA does not provide specific guidelines for creating posters. For this reason, the display of posters at conferences and professional meetings can vary quite a bit from poster to poster. Although the APA does not provide specific guidelines, we can identify many strategies you can use to get your poster noticed using the following suggestions adapted, in part, from Block (1996):

- Keep the title short. The title should clearly identify the topic of your poster and should be the largest font size you use. If needed, shorten the title in order to increase the font size of the title.

- Do not use a small font size, and use a consistent font type. The font size should not be smaller than 20 points, and the font type should be the same for the entire poster (except possibly the title). Larger font size and consistent font type is good because it makes a poster easy to read from at least 4 feet away.

- Use colorful figures and borders. A colorful display is eye-catching; however, keep the color simple by using solid colors throughout.

- Display the logo for your school affiliation (optional). Displaying your school logo is a point of pride and a way to advertise to others where the research was conducted.

- Place each text box or section in a logical order. The sections in a poster include the title, the abstract or overview, the method and results, figures and tables, conclusions or implications, and a list of key references. Try to organize each section, moving from left to right, in the same way that it would be presented in an APA-style manuscript.

- Make sure the poster takes less than 5 minutes to read. A poster does not need to be comprehensive; it needs to give enough information such that the reader can understand the gist of what you did and what you found.

- Avoid technical jargon. Do not assume that everyone in the audience is an expert. Avoid using words that are specific to your area of research, or if you do use these words, then define them in your poster. Make the poster accessible to a large audience.

- Always stand near the poster, but not directly in front of it. Stay near the poster to let people know that you are available to answer questions or talk about what you did, and stand away from it so that all patrons can clearly see the poster. Also, wait for the audience to address you with questions, and be respectful when you do respond to questions.

- Bring supportive materials, such as reprints or a printed copy of the poster itself, to give to attendees. This gives people something to bring home that will remind them of the poster you presented. Also, bring business cards so people can contact you if they have any follow-up questions after the poster session.

Most authors now use a single slide in Microsoft® PowerPoint to create their poster. Directions for using this software to create a poster are given in Appendix A.4. Sample posters that have been presented at professional conferences are also provided in Appendix A.4. Learning how to create a poster and following the suggestions provided in this section can help you make a strong impression at a poster session.

15.8 Giving a Professional Talk

The third method of communication introduced in this chapter is a professional talk. A talk is typically given in a formal setting. Graduate students often present their current work in brown-bag sessions to members of their department. At a doctoral level, researchers can be invited to present their work in a talk at conferences and professional meetings. The advantage of giving a talk is that the presenter is likely the only presenter or one of only a few presenters for the hour or so that the talk is given. By contrast, hundreds or thousands of authors present a poster in a single poster session. For this reason, giving a professional talk can be a great way to reach an engaged audience and promote your research, identify the scientific merits of your research, and even get people excited about your research.

There are many good suggestions for giving a professional talk. The following is a list of eight suggestions for giving an effective talk:

- Arrive early and be prepared. Being on time is the same as being late. You will need time to prepare, practice, and set up any technology, such as Microsoft® PowerPoint, needed to give the talk. As a general rule, always arrive about 30 minutes early to make sure everything is prepared so that you can start on time.

- Dress appropriately. Be aware of the audience and forum in which you are presenting. Try not to overdress (too formal) or underdress (too informal), but, when in doubt, overdress.

- Introduce yourself. Begin any talk with a brief introduction. State your name, affiliation, and general area of interest in an effort to relate to the audience and help the listeners understand who you are.

- Begin with an attention-grabber. A great talk captures the attention of an audience. Begin with a story, a short video clip, an exercise, a demonstration, or fun facts that get the audience interested to hear more. For example, if you give a talk on addiction, you could begin by describing a special case of a patient with the addiction and symptoms you plan to talk about.

- Use technology to facilitate your talk; do not read from it. Many presentations are given using Microsoft® PowerPoint. Do not read the slides verbatim; it reflects poorly on your preparedness and level of understanding of the topic of your talk. Instead, use only a few bulleted words on each slide, talk in your own words, and refer only to the slides as a reference for the order in which you present the topics of your talk. The more you engage the audience (and not the slides), the more effective the talk will be.

- Keep the talk focused. A talk is typically given within a specified time limit that is usually not more than 1 hour. Practice giving your talk often and keep to that script as closely as possible during the talk. Stay on topic so that you can stay on time. If an audience member asks an off-topic question or a question that will take too much time to answer, then let the individual know that the question is important to you and that it may be best for you to answer that question at the end of the talk. This allows you to show respect for the audience member and also allows you to keep the talk on topic and on time.

- Follow through with questions. Many questions can be answered during or immediately after a talk. However, if you do not know an answer to a question or did not get a chance to answer a specific question, then offer to take down the contact information of the person who asked the question so that you can follow up later with an answer. Make sure you follow through.

- Always end with references and acknowledgments. The speaker may have been invited to talk, and many people often help a speaker prepare a talk, so these people should be acknowledged. In addition, any work cited in the talk should be recognized at the end of the talk. If the talk is given using Microsoft® PowerPoint slides, then the final slide should list the references and acknowledgments.

The best advice of all is to relax and enjoy the moment. Public speaking tends to be stressful for many people. Breathe deeply, squeeze a stress ball, or tell yourself a joke. Do anything to relax and overcome any anxiety or stress you may be experiencing prior to a talk. For most talks, the audience is voluntary; by being present at your talk, your listeners have already expressed an interest in your topic. Following the guidelines described in this section, you can give a talk that appeals to your audience and allows you to present yourself as an authoritative, yet engaged, speaker.

LEARNING CHECK 5 ✓

1. What is a poster session?

2. What guidelines does the APA provide for creating a poster?

3. What is the advantage of giving a professional talk compared to presenting a poster?

Answers: 1. A poster session is a 1- to 4-hour time slot during which many authors stand near their poster ready and open to answer questions or talk about their work with interested attendees; 2. None; 3. The advantage of giving a talk is that, unlike in a poster session, the speaker is likely the only presenter or one of only a few presenters at the time the talk is given.

CHAPTER SUMMARY

LO 1 Identify three methods of communication among scientists.

- Three methods of communication among scientists are to publish a manuscript, present a poster, and give a talk.

LO 2 Describe three elements of communication.

- Three elements in communication are the speaker or author, the audience, and the message. The speaker or author uses first person and third person appropriately; uses past, present, and future tense appropriately; uses an impersonal writing style; reduces biased language; and gives credit where appropriate. The audience includes scientists and professionals, college students, and the general public. The message should be novel (contribute new findings or new ideas), interesting (to the readership of the work), and informative.

LO 3 Apply APA writing style and language guidelines for writing a manuscript.

- To submit a work for consideration for publication in a peer-reviewed journal, we prepare an APA-style manuscript using the writing style format described in the *Publication Manual*. Four writing and language guidelines for writing an APA-style manuscript are to be accurate; comprehensive, yet concise; conservative; and appropriate. To be comprehensive, yet concise, apply the following suggestions: Abbreviate where appropriate, display data in a figure or table, keep the writing focused, and do not repeat information.

LO 4 Apply APA formatting requirements for writing a manuscript.

- An APA-style manuscript is formatted or organized into the following major sections: title page, abstract, main body (includes introduction, methods, results, and discussion), references, footnotes (if any), tables (if any), figures (if any), and appendices (if any).

- A title page is on page 1 and includes the title, authors, affiliations, and author note. On page 2, the abstract provides a brief written summary of the purpose, methods, and results of a work or published document in 150 to 250 words. On page 3, the main body begins with the title on line 1, and the introduction begins on line 2. The introduction states a problem and why it is important to address, reviews the pertinent literature, and states how the problem will be addressed. The "Method" section is divided into four main subheadings: "Participants," "Procedures" (can be further divided into subheadings), "Data Analyses" (may be optional), and "Results." The "Discussion" section evaluates and interprets how the outcomes in a study relate to the problem that was tested. The "References" section, which begins on a new page, is an alphabetical list of all sources cited in a manuscript.

LO 5 Apply APA guidelines for writing and organizing a literature review article.

- A literature review article is a written comprehensive report of findings from previously published works about a problem in the form of a synthesis of previous articles or as a meta-analysis. To write the main body of a literature review:
  - o Identify the problem and how it will be evaluated.
  - o Integrate the literature to identify the state of the research.
  - o Identify how findings and interpretations in the published literature are related or consistent, or are inconsistent, contradictory, or flawed.
  - o Consider the progress made in an area of research and potential next steps toward clarifying the problem.

LO 6 Delineate how results are reported for a qualitative versus a quantitative research design.

- The "Results" section is replaced with an "Analysis" section in a qualitative research study, which provides a series of interpretations and contributes a new perspective or generates the possibility that many different perspectives can explain the observations made. The "Analysis" section is written as a narrative, and not as a report of statistical outcomes.

- In a qualitative report, the introduction and the "Method" section argue approaches to examining a problem in a way that often leaves open many alternatives that were anticipated or not anticipated by the authors. In the "Analysis" section, a narrative is used to describe what was observed, and the "Discussion" section evaluates possible explanations for those observations with little effort to generalize beyond the specific observations made.

LO 7 State APA guidelines for identifying the authorship of published scientific work.

- According to the APA, authors listed on the title page of a manuscript should be listed in order of their "relative scientific or professional contributions." The APA suggests that to resolve any concerns regarding authorship, all potential authors should talk about publication credit as early as possible.

LO 8 Identify guidelines for effectively presenting a poster.

- A poster is a concise description of a research study in the form of a display of text boxes, figures, and tables on a single large page. A poster is presented at a conference or professional meeting in a poster session, which is a 1- to 4-hour time slot during which many authors stand near their poster ready and open to answer questions or talk about their work with interested attendees.

- The APA does not provide specific guidelines for creating and presenting posters; however, using the following suggestions is advisable: Keep the title short, do not use small font size and use a constant font type, use colorful figures and borders, display the logo for your school affiliation, place each text box or section in a logical order, make sure the poster takes less than 5 minutes to read, avoid technical jargon, always stand near the poster but not directly in front of it, and bring supportive materials.

LO 9 Identify guidelines for effectively giving a professional talk.

- Giving a professional talk can be a great way to promote your research and get people excited about your work. The following is a list of eight suggestions for giving an effective talk: Arrive early and be prepared, dress appropriately, introduce yourself, begin with an attention-grabber, use technology to facilitate your talk, keep the talk focused, follow through with questions, and always end with references and acknowledgments.

KEY TERMS

peer review   literature review article   poster session

APA-style manuscript   poster

REVIEW QUESTIONS

1. State three methods of communication among scientists.

2. State three elements of communication.

3. Scientific journals use a peer review process to determine whether to accept or reject a manuscript for publication. What is peer review?

4. State the writing and language guideline for writing an APA-style manuscript (be accurate; be comprehensive, yet concise; be conservative; or be appropriate) that is described by each of the following:

   A. Proofread your manuscript before submitting it.

   B. Abbreviate where appropriate.

   C. Do not generalize beyond the data.

   D. Capitalize the word "Black" to refer to a social or ethnic group.

5. State the major sections in an APA-style manuscript in order of how each section should appear in the manuscript.

6. A researcher reports that students spent significantly more time attending to a passage given in color than when it was presented in black and white, $t(30) = 4.16, p < .05$. In which section of an APA-style manuscript do we report this outcome?

7. What information is conveyed in the introduction of an APA-style manuscript?

8. What sections constitute the first two pages of an APA-style manuscript?

9. What is the goal of a literature review?

10. In a qualitative report, the "Results" section is omitted and replaced with what section?

11. At what stage in the publication process should potential authors talk about publication credit?

12. How should the sections in a poster be organized, moving from left to right?

ACTIVITIES

1. Conduct a literature search and choose one article that interests you. After reading the article, write a three- to four-page paper that identifies whether each of the following was a strength or weakness in the introduction and discussion sections of the article, and give an example to support each argument:

   A. Did the introduction: Describe the problem and explain why it is important to conduct new research to address the problem? Integrate previous research that is relevant to the research conducted to address the problem? State the hypotheses being tested and the research design being used to address the problem?

   B. Did the discussion: State whether the findings lend support or nonsupport for the hypothesis that was tested? Give context for how the findings fit with previously published studies? Identify potential limitations of the research and methods, imprecision of measures that may have biased the pattern of results observed, and any potential threats to internal or external validity? Provide a broad summary or commentary on the importance of the findings?

2. Conduct a literature review and find one article that interests you. Create a poster for the study that is described in the article by applying the suggestions introduced for creating posters in Section 15.7.

Your Dissertation Module: Frequently Asked Questions

Harrison, E. and Rentzelas, P.

How will I be allocated to a supervisor?

The allocation process normally begins in late spring, when you will be asked to submit a choice form with your project ideas and preferred supervisor(s). You will have the opportunity to speak to staff members about your ideas during an open office afternoon, prior to submitting your choices. Allocations are then made based on topic choices and supervisor availability.

I didn't get allocated to my chosen supervisor, should I be worried?

No. All staff are experienced academics with extensive experience supervising dissertation projects in all areas of psychology. It is not essential for your supervisor to be an expert in your chosen topic. There are a number of reasons why you might not have been allocated to your chosen supervisor(s). If you are concerned you can speak to the module coordinators.

What sort of support will my supervisor provide?

Your supervisor's role is to oversee the general process of conducting a dissertation project. They are not there to do the work for you, but will be able to offer advice on research design, appropriate methodology, ethical considerations, data analysis, and writing up the dissertation.

How often should I see my supervisor?

You can see your supervisor as often as you like, but remember that you are only allowed 4 hours of contact time across the module – use it wisely! You can also use your supervision time for skype meetings, email contact, etc. if you are unable to meet face-to-face.

Is 4 hours of supervision enough, and how can I use it effectively?

Yes, 4 hours is plenty. It is expected that you will use around an hour of this time when preparing the proposal. The proposal is essentially a plan of your project, and getting started can often require a lot of supervision. As module leaders, we would encourage you to break down the rest of your supervision time so that you can meet with your supervisor about each of the following areas for approximately 30 minutes each: the literature review, the methodology, data collection preparation, data analysis, the results chapter, and preparing the final dissertation. Note that this is just a suggestion, and your use of supervision time is flexible – everyone is different. For example, some students may feel they need more support on the write up, whereas some students may need more support with the data analysis.

What happens if I miss any formative deadlines?

The formative deadlines are set to structure the module and enable you to manage your time effectively so that you are only working on one section at a time. If you feel that you are unable to meet the formative deadlines for any reason, you should contact your supervisor and arrange additional time. It is important that this is done *before* the deadlines though, as otherwise your supervisor may not be able to schedule time to provide you with any formative feedback.

Who will mark my work?

Your supervisor will be the first marker for both summative assessments, and will work closely with an allocated second marker to agree on a suitable mark. Your supervisor will also provide formative feedback on any formative sections submitted.

How do I work out my module mark?

The proposal is worth 20% of the module mark, and the final dissertation is worth 80%. Take the mark for the proposal and multiply it by 0.2, then take the mark for the final dissertation and multiply this by 0.8, then add the two values together.